Achieving

Authentic Success™

Make Things Happen

Achieve Personal Significance

X Out the Negatives

Internalize Right Principles

March to a Mission

Integrate All of Life

Zero In on Caring for People

Energize Internally

Realign Rigorously

Stay the Course

10 Timeless Life Principles That Will Maximize Your <u>Real</u> Potential

Authored By:

Dr. Ron Jenson

Published By:

Future Achievement International®
P.O. 891345
Temecula, CA 92589-1345

ISBN 0-9709483-4-4

(858) 487-3177
www.futureachievement.com

Special Thanks

To some of those special people who have helped me achieve authentic success:

My mom, Maxine,
Who taught me to work hard

My dad, Bob,
who models gentleness

My wife, Mary
Who makes daily living a delight

My son, Matt
Who helps me build "straight lines" in my life

My daughter, Molly,
Who makes life fun

My longtime friend, Bob Safford,
Who keeps "making things happen"

My inner-life mentor, Bill Bright,
Who best models to me the power of "energizing the inner life"

My friend, Kevin Jenkins,
Who illustrates daily the ability to adjust to changing situations

My partners, Doug Tucker and Greg Dolby,
Who have provided me with new understanding
of the concept of "faithfulness

And my associates over the years
who have grappled with and sought to model "authentic success"

What Others Are Saying About Dr. Ron Jenson...

"Dr. Ron Jenson's approach to leadership is what companies are really needing. I have seen him with top worldwide business leaders and what he has written really works and helps people win big. Very Big."

Dr. Ken Blanchard, Best Selling Author
The One-Minute Manager, Speaker

"Achieving Authentic Success provides specific inspirational direction for those who seek to win in all areas of life. Informative and practical... is loaded with common sense and the realistic side of inspiration. GOOD stuff!"

Zig Ziglar, Chairman
The Zig Ziglar Corporation

"Ron's proven approach to leadership training makes the reality of a fulfilling and successful life available to everyone. He presents these timeless principles professionally, yet practically in a down to earth way that is easy to understand and put into practice. His message is greatly needed throughout our world today."

Norm Miller, Chairman
Interstate Batteries

"Dr. Jenson has written a comprehensive and do-able achievement program for following through with one's personal and professional goals with emphasis on inner success versus outward success."

Joe Gibbs, Former Head Coach
Washington Redskins; Joe Gibbs Racing

Ron Jenson has taken ten very practical, individual skills and shown how they are foundational to building authentically successful and effective lives. The book really challenged me in many areas of my life. I am going to be recommending it widely."

Pat Williams, COO /General Manager
Orlando Magic, National Basketball Association

"I felt the content of your book, Achieving Authentic Success, is not only timely for me at this point in my career, but for our entire organization and the nation as a whole. The life skills and action steps you are presenting will help everyone build an outstanding foundation for a truly successful life."

Hugh Maclellan, Jr., Chairman of the Executive Committee
Provident Companies

"Your insights...hit home. Numerous people responded relating a changed perspective in their lives as a result of the message."
David Hentschel, Chairman, Occidental Oil and Gas Corporation

"Your approach has been practical, convincing and relevant to the real world. I, along with hundreds of key business leaders across our nation, have benefited significantly from the powerful thrust of your efforts."
Dick Capen, U.S. Ambassador to Spain, former Vice Chairman, Knight Ridder, Inc.

"You reminded me how important it is to keep our priorities straight and to actively plan for a 'balanced life'. It was easy to see how 'success' often leads us away from that objective—to our detriment. Your talk really stimulated me to reevaluate my own priorities and be more conscious of my daily decisions."
Mary Walker, Former Partner at Luce Forward Hamilton & Scripps

"I have witnessed your ability to work with top political, professional, and executive leaders on an international basis. You are one of the most effective communicators that I know."
The Honorable Bob McEwen, former US Congressman, OH

"For the past 30 years, I have worked for a multi-national, international bank as a corporate executive in several countries. During that time, I have been to several professional training programs but I have found this program makes a real difference. The MAXIMIZERS change you from the inside out in terms of your professional, family and personal life. I recommend this program."
Abdul Latif, Asia Development Bank

"Never in modern history have moral standards and non-negotiables been more important than today."
Dr. D. S. Reimer, Reimer Express World Corp.

"Build an organization that lives these principles and you will have a successful company-- for generations to come."
Bunker Hunt, International Businessman

"The MAXIMIZERS principles are for people to be able to develop their highest potential while at the same time supporting and leading other people."
Stan Smith, Professional Tennis Champion.

Future Achievement International®

Personal Leadership Solutions...

The Vision

Dr. Jenson is the Chairman and Co-founder of Future Achievement International. Future Achievement and its strategic partnerships are committed to impacting and changing lives by sharing and teaching a set of universal life principles, which will have a dramatic effect on individuals, families, youth, business and non-profit organizations, educational institutions, government and communities at large.

You Can Make A Difference

We encourage you to study the principles within this book and make them part and parcel to your life. Visit our website to review other educational learning materials that can help you impact your co-workers...your family...your children...and your community at large!

www.futureachievement.com

Achieving Authentic Success™

Table Of Contents

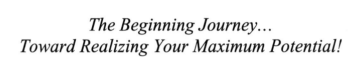

The Beginning Journey...
Toward Realizing Your Maximum Potential!

Preface

This easy-to-read book addresses the feelings, longings, and emotions felt by many professionals and business people in today's busy, challenging world.   It is our application of the ten life principles developed by Dr. Ron Jenson called MAXIMIZERS™. Incorporating these principles into careers, dreams and relationships will bring great rewards of personal growth, life balance, productivity, happiness and peace of mind.

This book has been inspired and written by Dr. Ron Jenson the Chairman and Co-founder of Future Achievement International®. He encourages you to take his MAXIMIZERS principles, build them into your life and communicate them directly to others.

The leadership gurus Jim Collins and Daniel Goleman say that future successful leaders must demonstrate "intense professional will and personal humility" along with "emotional intelligence." They have aptly articulated the problem.   Dr. Jenson provides the solution as he explains how to build those qualities into your life.

Many individuals around the world have incorporated these principles with powerful and encouraging results. We are constantly hearing such comments as,

"This is changing my life."

"I now have hope for the future."

"I have learned how to actually change through building good habits."

"Now I can resolve conflict the right way."

"I'm now experiencing much greater peace."

"I'm much more productive at work."

People have gained a great deal of self-fulfillment in the past few decades, as the world of professional opportunities has opened to so many. Now is the time to sort out the successes in your life where you have played to your strengths and move in a direction of *achieving authentic success* with these 10 lifetime principles.

It's essential to understand how the MAXIMIZERS will work in your life to take you each day into exciting adventures and opportunities. Study these marvelous insights that make it a possible and certainly a worthy endeavor.

This book lays before you a feast of ideas and solutions to make your life a powerhouse of personal growth, respect, caring, impact, productivity and satisfaction. These insights into success begin in the opening chapter with a discussion of the true meaning of success. Each chapter builds on that definition and the book concludes with a strong push for staying the course.

Dr. Jenson and his company, Future Achievement International, teach these principles all around the world in multiple languages and geographic areas (over 40 countries). We encourage you to not only read this book, but study it and then visit their website futureachievement.com, to order other resource materials that will help you build an even more solid foundation, leading to authentic success and significance in every area of your life.

As you read this book, take time to respond to, on paper, the many *Action Steps* that are incorporated into each chapter. They will lead you to test your knowledge and understanding of the excellent things you are doing already and encourage you to improve those areas that need work.

These points of improvement are, as Dr. Ken Blanchard states, "...principles that really work and help people win big." So, read them carefully and begin to incorporate the MAXIMIZERS as part of your very being.

In a day when world cultures are rapidly falling apart, we desperately need to learn again how to live life to its fullest. You can make a difference in your company...your family...your community ...and the culture at large!

We encourage you to *learn* the principles shared in this book, then *apply* these principles in your everyday personal and professional life, and then to teach these principles to those that you influence.

You Can Make A Difference!

The Foundation

Everyone has a definition of success. We may not be able to articulate it or write it down. But we are *always* trying to succeed at something. That "something," whatever it is, drives our thoughts, feelings, and actions.

We are constantly focused on what we want to accomplish, whether we realize it or not. Our concept of success has been developed and conditioned over the years by the media, family upbringing, peers and associates, and various experiences. The net effect can be either positive or negative.

Therefore, the questions to ask yourself are: What are you trying to accomplish? How will you know if you have succeeded once you "get there"? And, moreover, can you *ever* "get there" or is it all just a process?

How Are You Defining Success?

Power? Is power the secret to success? Hitler had a lot of power, but calling him a success would be to condone his actions! Think about the stories Wall Street provides. There are hundreds of "successful" businesspeople with enormous power—along with broken marriages, failing families, and ruined reputations. The common philosophy is that if you're going to succeed in business, you have to forfeit success in other areas of life. I don't buy that.

Prosperity? Materialism is a major problem today. Yet possessing things and having money aren't wrong. It is only when we become preoccupied with those things that we begin to miss the purpose and meaning of life.

The January 28, 1960, issue of *The Washington Post* records a letter from author John Steinbeck, to politician Adlai Stevenson. Steinbeck wrote, "A strange species we are. We can stand anything God and nature throw at us save only plenty. If I wanted to destroy a nation, I would give it too much and I would have it on its knees: miserable, greedy, and sick."

Position? Some people say that position defines success. Ferdinand and Imelda Marcos had prominent positions in the world. But did they succeed? It all depends on your definition of success.

I have a friend who was a U.S. congressman. This senior senator was always my choice for President, but he never ran. During a visit to his office, I saw many of the "hate letters" he'd received displayed on his bulletin board. Underneath those letters was a quotation from the Bible: "Woe to you when all men speak well of you" (Luke 6:26).

This great man had enough humility and wisdom to know that a responsible position inevitably carries with it substantial criticism, both fair and unfair. Therefore, position alone isn't a worthy measuring stick for success.

Prestige? Being known and recognized? Many people who have it can tell you that prestige can be very fleeting. Baseball star Pete Rose was a man of prestige at one moment and a man of notoriety the next.

Prestige certainly is no guarantee of success. In fact, those who have prestige normally receive an equal or even greater amount of denigration.

Pleasure? "The rule of life is to make business a pleasure, and pleasure our *only* business," said Aaron Burr. This aptly conveys the rampant attitude of pleasure seeking in our day and age.

Widespread as this desire for pleasure is, and as well documented in our day and age in particular books such as *Through the Culture of Narcissism,* there is nothing new about it. It's simply a form of hedonism.

Hedonism, a philosophical worldview in which the experience and appreciation of pleasure are the highest goals, has been around since the beginning of time. Aristippus (435–356 B.C.), whose motto "Eat, drink, and be merry, for tomorrow you die," could also fit the pleasure seekers of the new millennium, was one of the early advocates of hedonism. To be a hedonist is to make a god out of pleasure.

Building a life around self-focused pleasure is simply not satisfying in the long run. You can easily see the problem. People put all their eggs in one basket to chase the five Ps to find success...

> ➢ *Power*
>
> ➢ *Prosperity*
>
> ➢ *Position*
>
> ➢ *Prestige*
>
> ➢ *Pleasure*

To be fair, the five P's don't always result in personal devastation. In fact, they are rather amoral—neither good nor bad in themselves. But their use or abuse determines the outcome of a person's life. I don't want to discourage you from enjoying the rewards of your hard work. I want to encourage you to leverage those rewards for the good of others and yourself.

What about you? What is your concept of success? Have you deliberately developed one, or has yours simply evolved through the influence of the culture around you? And is it the *right* concept of success?

Build Success in All Areas of Your Life

Any success you attain must be holistic success—that is, balanced, integrated success, one that is in harmony with who you are. I believe that if you succeed in work and yet fail in personal relationships, you haven't succeeded. And if you accomplish great things, but live miserably in the process, you haven't succeeded. Only a life rooted in *real and lasting values* is successful.

Think about it for a moment. You are a whole person. You have emotional, physical, volitional, spiritual, and relational sides to your being. Beyond that, you have responsibilities in various realms—business, family and community. Each of these areas has sub-responsibilities.

They are all interrelated. You cannot afford to succeed in your finances and yet fail in your marriage. You cannot achieve levels of excellence in your business and yet burn out physically and emotionally. You must be winning in all vital areas to be successful. You may be thinking, "But you can't have it all!" Oh, yes you can!

You were *meant* to have it all. The key is having it all *correctly*. Now if you're a business owner, this idea of holistic success might make you a little nervous. After all, if employees give attention to their personal lives, families, places of worship and communities, won't that hurt your bottom-line? No!

Not if you have defined your bottom line not only in fiscal terms, but also in human terms. You have to realize that a well-managed life produces a well-managed business. Happy and growing people are more productive; healthy families feed profitable ventures.

This reality has been driven home in recent days by author Jim Collins who says, "...the key to successful leadership is a matter of *intense professional will* and *intense personal humility.* You must have an iron will professionally and you must have humility."

In a similar vein, Daniel Goleman has written in his recent work, *Primal Leadership*, "Managing for financial results begins with the leader managing his or her inner life so that the right emotional and behavioral chain reaction occurs. Managing one's inner life is not easy. For many of us, it's our most difficult challenge." He goes on to say that this is all about personal and interpersonal skills or, to put it another way, personal leadership.

My goal is to help you with such skills as you refine, clarify, and articulate a definition of success that is in harmony with the real *you* and will allow you to lead a balanced, fulfilled, productive and significant life.

Success Depends on What *You* Do with *You*

Success is in your hands. Indeed, all success is based on the way you manage yourself. And the way you manage yourself is only as good as the principles upon which you build your life. Therefore, pursue *truth.* By that I mean universal truths. The tendency today is to elevate a relativistic mind set in which no absolutes exist. This viewpoint is nonsense. ***Absolute universal principles exist!***

Just as physical laws govern the physical universe, so universal principles govern human existence. If these laws are violated, inevitable repercussions result. These principles are abiding truths—universal, absolute, non-negotiable. They are as factual as the law of gravity.

We may not understand them or buy into them, but that doesn't invalidate them. They simply won't move; they are firm. Our choice is either to discover and fully embrace them and thereby succeed as we are meant to, or to ignore them and fail without ever knowing why.

If you want to succeed in life, you must passionately pursue the discovery of truth and know how to apply that truth appropriately in your life. This is called *wisdom*. The word *wisdom* in the original Hebrew language referred to craftsmanship. To be wise was to be a craftsman at living, an artisan of life. In short, that is what this book is all about.

✓ Assumption One: You are moving toward your definition of success.

✓ Assumption Two: Authentic success means maximizing all of your life and impact.

✓ Assumption Three: Wisely applying universal principles is the key to authentic success.

I am suggesting **10 Non-Negotiable Principles** that can serve as the organizing system around which you can develop all the subsequent truths that should flow in your life. These principles form the framework of the MAXIMIZERS acrostic that I will develop for you.

What does it mean to be a "Maximizer?" The best way to explain this is with an acrostic. Every letter stands for a phrase, and every phrase states a basic principle about life that I will develop more deeply in this book. Here is the easy-to-remember MAXIMIZERS acrostic:

M ake things happen

A chieve personal significance

X out the negatives

I nternalize right principles

M arch to a mission

I ntegrate all of life

Z ero in on caring for people

E nergize internally

R ealign rigorously

S tay the course

These ten MAXIMIZERS principles are grouped into three major categories:

> ➤ *Attitudes*
> ➤ *Beliefs*
> ➤ *Commitments*

The power of these three categories comes through aligning them together. Some people have good attitudes, but lack commitment and follow-through. Others have solid beliefs, but negative attitudes sabotage their authentic success. Still others are volitionally strong and can will themselves to accomplish things, but consistently fall short because either their belief systems or attitudes are inhibited. Finally, others may be solid in all three areas, but lack the integration of the ten MAXIMIZERS principles.

If you are going to authentically succeed, you must focus on the roots and not the fruit of your life. The fruit in your life includes happiness, fulfilling relationships, prosperity, influence, position, etc. The roots are the non-negotiable principles around which you build your life. If you feed these roots, the fruits will come.

These are the basic *attitudes, beliefs*, and *commitments* I will communicate and illustrate throughout this book via the MAXIMIZERS principles. The soil for those roots is wisdom or universal truths. Perhaps you have spent your life focusing on obtaining fruit. I urge you to stop. Make a commitment now to spend the rest of your life focusing on *roots*—those principles that when fully embraced produce authentic success.

Action Steps

(1) Take a few minutes to write your own obituary.

(2) How will you know you have succeeded at the end of your life?

(3) Rate yourself according to the MAXIMIZERS principles listed here in the form of a creed (1 is the lowest rating, 10 the highest):

MAXIMIZERS

Make things happen. I take charge of my life as a difference-maker.
1 . . . 5 . . . 10

Achieve personal significance. I live my life with a sense of destiny.
1 . . . 5 . . . 10

X-out the negatives. I embrace problems as positive opportunities.
1 . . . 5 . . . 10

Internalize right principles. I center my life on bedrock principles.
1 . . . 5 . . . 10

March to a mission. I passionately pursue my mission.
1 . . . 5 . . . 10

Integrate all of life. I keep all vital areas of my life in balance.
1 . . . 5 . . . 10

Zero in on caring for people. I put others first and serve them.
1 . . . 5 . . . 10

Energize internally. I cultivate my character and spirit.
1 . . . 5 . . . 10

Realign rigorously. I keep adjusting to needs.
1 . . . 5 . . . 10

Stay the course. I will never, ever, ever quit.
1 . . . 5 . . . 10

"Success is the progressive realization of all that you were meant to be and do."

Dr. Ron Jenson

Section 1

Root Attitudes

What you see is what you'll be!

This statement articulates the power of attitude. The following section of this book develops three "root attitudes" that individuals must develop if they are going to succeed in their lives and professions.

First, the foundational issue of taking responsibility for your life and *making things happen* will be addressed. As long as you live as a victim–one who is not responsible for his or her actions, and life in general–you are doomed to fail. But, if you take responsibility for your *attitudes, beliefs, and commitments,* you will achieve authentic success. You cannot control what has happened in the past or what others might think, feel, say or do. You cannot control the end results or fruits in your life. But you can take responsibility for planting good roots and nourishing them with the right tools. This *rightness living* ultimately produces the fruit of authentic success. But it requires that you take charge of your own life and accept responsibility for it.

The second root attitude is the principle of *achieving personal significance.* Your self-perception determines your behavior. If you see yourself as having a destiny and being of great value, you will act accordingly. The deep crises in America's inner cities and other troubled locations around the world would be greatly relieved if self-concept issues were dealt with in the right way. This chapter addresses how to change a faulty self-concept through healthy, balanced affirmation and through facing and addressing the reality of your soft spots or weak areas.

The third root attitude in this section is learning to *X-out the negatives.* Here we talk about how to handle problems. Do you run from them or see their value? We explain how to develop right beliefs toward critical areas in your life by destroying your fears, doubts, and other inhibitors.

Focus On The Roots...
Not on The Fruit!

1

Make Things Happen

How to be a Difference Maker

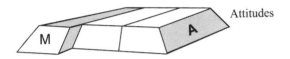

"The best years of your life are the ones in which you decide your problems are your own. You don't blame them on your mother, the ecology, or the president. You realize that you control your own destiny."

Psychologist Albert Ellis

A freshman at his first collegiate football practice broke away for an eighty-yard touchdown. His teammates looked at him in amazement and disbelief. His coach shouted, "Kid, you're going to have quite a future around here." Later, his excited, blonde girlfriend kissed him. His life at that moment was completely satisfying. His future bright!

Yet, nothing in that young man's life measured up to that football moment. He never made it to the big time as everyone thought he would. His business career, forget it. The marriage went sour. His life dragged. The pain of failures became even greater when he reflected on that perfect football day. That eighty yards was bitter sweet in his mind. Pleasant...but past.

Irwin Shaw poignantly illustrates our contemporary dilemma with that scenario. Many of us waste our lives struggling to either recapture moments we experienced in the past or stumble on to an elusive perfect future.

But waiting for something to come creeping around the corner is merely reacting to life.

If you are going to be a difference-maker, a *maximizer*, you have to be assertive and proactive in thought and action. You must *make things happen*. Stop letting things engulf you and take responsibility for your future now!

This is the beginning point of all success: You must *want to* control the things that determine your success or you will fail. You have to use your best reserve of brains, emotion, physical strength and spiritual enlightenment to drive your life in the direction of your success. If your foundational attitude is not firmly set in your mind, you may at times erupt in moments of brilliance and enlightenment, but you will never develop sound patterns of excellence and achievement.

A Civilization of Victims

Under pressure, people who merely react to life fall back into the "blame game."

We have become a civilization of blamers and victims. Look around. We blame our past, our genes, our parents, society, heritage, our "dysfunctionalities" and anything else we can think of for our existing personal problems. *And they are personal problems.* They are squarely inside of us. Not the person next to us.

In one of the most insightful books in recent years, *The Nation of Victims*, Charles Sykes delineates and documents the problem of victim mentality. Some of his points:

- An FBI agent embezzles two thousand dollars and subsequently loses it while gambling in Atlantic City. Though he is fired, he gets reinstated once he convinces the court that his tendency toward gambling with other people's money is a "handicap" and therefore protected under federal law.

- A young man steals a car from a parking lot. He's killed trying to escape. His family sues the proprietor of the parking lot for failing to prevent theft.

- A man admits to exposing himself more than ten thousand times (being convicted on more than thirty occasions). He's turned down for a job as a parking attendant because of his arrest record. What does he do? He sues based on the argument that he has never exposed himself in a parking lot. Other places, yes. Wisconsin employment officials agreed that the flasher was a victim of illegal job discrimination.

As absurd as such stories are, the fact is they are happening in increasing numbers with the fires fanned by tabloids and television that pander to the "victimized." The explosive rise in litigation, coupled with extremist psychologists and attorneys, helps create a dysfunctional society.

Though there are support groups that are undeniably helpful, these groups must guard against encouraging participants to blame others and not take responsibility for their own lives.

Think about the constant headlines today involving corporate ethical breakdowns. Major corporate leaders are accused of cooking the books. Conflicts of interest seem to abound with few taking responsibility for their actions and their positions.

You cannot afford to be a *victim*. No matter how much you may feel like a victim or enjoy the sympathy of others, you must take the initiative and make a difference with your life. That is your destiny!

Be Proactive, Not Reactive

Take responsibility for your thoughts and your actions and grasp the future you want for yourself. You cannot sit around and wait for life to find you. You have to go get it. If you really care to make a difference you need to go after what you want.

My good friend and a successful entrepreneur, Beverly Sallee, shared a story with me recently about her friend Renee. Her life illustrates the importance of not sitting around. Renee faced her circumstances head on…with a vengeance!

Renee had the world securely in the palm of her hand. She was young and vibrant and each day shared her passion for music with young people as a choir director in a Southern California high school. She was also planning a wedding: her wedding. She didn't know what challenges each new day would bring, but good things were happening. Her future was filled with promise. Each day was exciting to her.

That all changed, literally, overnight. Two months before her wedding Renee fell out of bed in a freak accident and instantly became a quadriplegic. When her fiancé heard the news he prayed, "Lord, don't let her die. I don't care if there is a wheel chair, just don't let her die." When he came to her hospital room he smiled and said, "Hi honey, we can do this." Renee smiled back and said, "I guess we'll always have a good parking space." One year later they were married.

It was her attitude that made all the difference. Good things had been happening in Renee's life prior to her accident, but when the road became rocky she didn't lose heart or faith. Instead, she started to make things happen. She did not let the promise of her future elude her. She went after it with determination.

With the help of a vocal coach and friend Renee began to lift weights on her diaphragm. After a five-month stay in the hospital she was able to lift 55 pounds, thus enabling her to sing again. Soon she was again sharing her passion for music with young people as the director of the Children's Choir at the mission in San Juan Capistrano. She recorded several albums and began traveling to give concerts. In 1995 she was able to deliver a child.

Today, Renee continues to sing and raise her family. Each day she wheels her son, Daniel, into class on the back of her wheelchair. Life is different than she ever expected, but Renee didn't stop living because good things stopped happening. No, with a healthy attitude and the support of friends and family, she started to make things happen. Good things, life-changing things, things that make it worth waking up each morning just to see what is going to happen next.

Here is the first key to success: When you take control of the things in your life that determine authentic success, then you will step onto the path of achieving your goals. *You will become proactive!*

I work with one Fortune 400 construction management company that has what they call the 51% rule as a core value. Their point is that it is always 51% of YOUR responsibility to solve a problem if you are aware of it. In other words, don't say it's not my job." Instead, be proactive and make things happen. Take the initiative.

Your decision to take charge of your life is the very seed of your success. Another way of saying "taking charge" is "being proactive." This word—*proactive*—is a simple combination of two familiar words: *pro*, meaning "for," and *active,* meaning "doing something." In other words: *Don't just sit there—do something!*

You and I get into trouble routinely by focusing on things over which we have little or no control. Will this meeting be positive? Will my child be safe? Will people like me? Will I close the sale? Will I be happy?

This is the *fruit* of your life, the result of how you're living. It does no good to focus on the fruit. In fact, it can be harmful, often resulting in worry, fear, manipulation…and worse.

Instead, you need to focus on those things you can control: the *roots* of your life—**right attitudes, right beliefs, and right commitments.** By so doing, you will use your emotional energy in a positive way and actually move forward more quickly. This proactive method does make a difference.

Reactive people focus on the *fruit* (results). Proactive people focus on the *roots* (principles). **The choice is yours…**

Will you see yourself as a victim, who only reacts? Or, as a victorious fighter who is in control and driving toward success?

Psychologists tell us that stress is a natural reality. Stress is tension that comes into our lives as part of the process of living. We can respond to stress in two ways: as a victim, who acts in a distressful (inappropriate) way, or as a victor, who acts in an appropriate way. If we respond appropriately, we can control stress and increase our capability for greater energy and a positive outcome. It takes discipline.

Be Disciplined…

We begin to make things happen when we become *disciplined.* We don't accomplish anything in this life without self-discipline. Richard Shelley Taylor, in his book *The Disciplined Life*, defines self-discipline this way:

"The ability to regulate conduct by principle and judgment rather than impulse, desire, high pressure, or social custom."

Now here's a question for you. Are there habits in your life that were acceptable when you were a child but aren't acceptable now? Are you still struggling with giving in to impulse?

Everyone struggles with one or more of three areas: pride, sensualism, and greed. Pride, which has its place, is unhealthy when it is stimulated by self-absorption. Sensualism, while positive when we're enjoying good music and good food, is being *preoccupied* with sensual fulfillment—food, sex, sound, and thrill seeking. (Many commercials and advertisements today are geared toward sensualism.)

Greed doesn't have a good side. Greed is wanting more just because it's there. Hand in hand with greed goes covetousness, that is, wanting what belongs to someone else. Greed and covetousness create a generation of people who live on credit and can't stop spending.

Discipline is the ability to *consciously control* your reaction to your life and circumstances. It is the ability to put first things first. Without it, you react to life rather than taking charge of it.

...Not Lazy

Listen to this old proverb: "Take a lesson from the ants, you sluggard (lazy fellow). Learn from their ways and be wise: for though they have no king to make them work, yet they labor hard all summer, gathering food for the winter. But you—all you do is sleep. When will you wake up? 'Let me sleep a little longer!' Sure, just a little more! And as you sleep, poverty creeps upon you like a robber and destroys you."

Compare the ant to the sloth. According to *How to Conquer Slothfulness*, European explorers discovered the sloth and gave it a name that embodied the characteristic and even the sound of the Hebrew word "atsluwth," which means, "to be idle."

The sloth is the embodiment of idleness. It can spend an entire lifetime in a single tree. In fact, it's the slowest of all mammals. It's estimated that a sloth can only move a few feet in one minute. One scientist observed that the cellular fluids of a single-celled protozoon move faster than a sloth trying to escape from a python.

The sloth is simply a lazy creature. As a result of its motionlessness, a sloth with its long coarse hair becomes infested with moths. Algae often grow on a sloth to the extent that the animal can take on a blue-green appearance and gives off a distinct odor.

When it comes to food the sloth simply maintains its plumpness by eating through the forest right around it. If food becomes at all scarce, a sloth will go hungry. That's why sloths are extremely susceptible to drought, fires, insect invasions, and so on.

Many scientists maintain that a sloth will die of starvation if food is not within immediate grasp. This is why the fossil record indicates that there are ten times as many extinct species of sloths as living ones.

Now compare the sloth to the ant. Even though the queen ant is the mother and the center attraction in an ant colony, she's really not the chief ruler. Instead there are older ants that serve as leaders by example. They show the younger ones what to do. There are no supervisors, chiefs, or officers among these ants.

The way worker ants provide food is to leave a trail of drops that contain a scent common to the whole colony. Other workers follow the trail and that's how they find their source of food. In an ant colony there really are no "poor" ants. These little insects share their food by storing it before it's digested in what's called a "social stomach." Those who have abundance give voluntarily to those who have less so they all might share equally. These ants actually work during the summer time because their bodies are affected by cool weather. As the nests cool in the fall, the ants become weaker and ultimately begin hibernation in the coldest months. In order for them to survive during that cold time, they must work hard during the spring and summer.

Now consider what the ants have against them. Most ants have compound eyes. They see a mosaic rather than a single image and, in fact, beyond more than an inch, the ant is virtually blind, except for an awareness of some degree of light or darkness.

Ants, like other insects, also have no ears. And even though they're exceedingly small, an ant can carry up to 50 times its weight over 100 yards. That's equivalent to a 200-pound man carrying over five tons on his back for a distance of 17 miles.

These industrious little insects often will make as much as four round trips a day to various food sources that may be over four hundred feet from their nest. This is equivalent to a man walking 68 miles. And these ants move quickly. One estimate is that if an ant were capable of a man's stride, his normal walking speed would be 20 miles per hour.

One other interesting insight about the ant is that he can work for years without wearing out. Whereas bees live for only five or six weeks before they work themselves to death, an ant can work for over six years and continue to maintain a high level of efficiency.[i]

Which one of these critters best reflects your life?

1. Work Hard

If you're going to succeed in life, you must work hard. Indeed, this work ethic must be reflected in every critical area of your life. There simply is no shortcut.

Gary Player won more international golf tournaments in his day than anyone else. Today he's still winning on the Seniors tour, and winning big. Throughout his career, people have said to him, "I'd give anything if I could hit the golf ball like you."

On one particularly tough day, Player was tired and frustrated when once again he heard that comment: "I'd give anything if I could hit the ball just like you." Player's usual politeness failed him as he replied tersely to the spectator, "No you wouldn't. You'd give anything to hit a golf ball like me *if it was easy.*

"Do you know what you've got to do to hit a golf ball like me? You've got to get up at five o'clock in the morning every day, go out on the course, and hit one thousand golf balls. Your hand starts bleeding, you walk up to the clubhouse, wash the blood off your hand, slap a bandage on it, and go out and hit another thousand golf balls. That's what it takes to hit a golf ball like me."

A comment by Thomas Paine is so telling:

"That which we obtain too easily we esteem too lightly."

If you actually value something, you've got to work hard at it. You must work hard in your business, work hard in your family, and work hard at personal fitness, faith, and friendship. Every area of your life needs this discipline!

"Without work," said Albert Camas, "all life becomes rotten." But with work and hard effort, life becomes meaningful and exciting.

2. Develop Right Habits

Aristotle was right: *"Excellence is not just an act but a habit."*

Robert Ringer, in his excellent book *Million Dollar Habits*, builds his thesis around this concept of habits. One of his first premises is that success does not depend upon superior intelligence, special skills, formal education, luck, etc.

He states, "The world is saturated with intelligent, highly educated, extraordinarily skilled people who experience ongoing frustration because of their lack of success. Millions of others spend their lives working hard, long hours only to die broke."

He writes, "Success is a matter of understanding and religiously practicing specific, simple habits that *always* lead to success."

Ringer then makes these telling statements:

"Remember, life is nothing more than the sum total of many successful years.

...A successful year is nothing more than the sum total of many successful months.

...A successful month is nothing more than the sum total of many successful weeks.

...A successful week is nothing more than the sum total of many successful days!"

That's why practicing successful habits day in and day out is the most certain way to win over the long term.

If you want to be excellent, you have to develop the habit of being excellent by doing the right things over and over and over.

Let's say you have a problem with your tongue—you talk behind people's backs. You have to develop the habit of saying positive things about them. Or, if you have problems not getting the job done because of laziness or procrastination, practice completing things over and over until you develop the habit of finishing them.

You must begin with the desire to succeed. What is the specific habit you want to build? If you have no idea where to start, ask your spouse or a close friend. He or she knows you best.

Ask yourself why you want to build a particular habit. Write out clearly what you gain or what you lose by practicing or not practicing this habit. If you don't attach enough pain to quitting a bad habit, or enough pleasure to practicing a good one, you'll not make the needed change. So, how do you develop habits? Here are several core competencies.

First, rehearse the new habit in your mind. Go through mental *repetition*. Habits are things we do without thinking about them. But we only get to that place of *mindless* habit after *mindful* repetition. For instance, when you button your shirt, do you button it up or down? Most of us could not answer that question without thinking about it because it's now a mindless, ingrained habit. But when we first learned to button our shirts as small children we concentrated. We focused. We thought about it. It was the beginning of the habit of our own unique way of getting dressed.

Imagine your mind as a great mountain. Attitudes you hold and habits you've developed are like little springs that flow down that mountain and over time become deep rivers. Habits are deep rivers that begin in your mind. They become actions that, under given circumstances, you fall into quite naturally. The encouraging news is that as you create new rivers of good, healthy habits the old ones will slowly fill up and fade away.

The second technique for developing good habits is *practice*. This moves the habit from the thinking level to the acting level. You have to understand up front that you're going to fail many times as you develop new habits. However, if you continue to practice a habit over and over—falling, picking yourself up, and trying again—after a period of time you'll have it down!

Many psychologists agree that if you can do something for twenty-one consecutive days, it becomes a habit. Add to that assurance the caution of William James: "Never suffer an exception to occur until the new habit is securely rooted in your life. Each lapse is like letting go of a ball of string which one is carefully winding up; a single slip undoes more than a great many turns will wind again."

A third technique to develop is a *feedback* mechanism. Monitor your growth. Take the new habit you want to develop and make a simple chart. Gauge yourself for twenty-one days, and mark when you are successful and when you aren't, when you fall back into a bad habit, and when you are victorious.

It's up to *you* whether you truly develop effective habits in an effort to correct past failures. The future is yours, but you have to make it happen.

Action Steps

1. How do you view yourself—as victim or victor? Do you believe you are stuck and helpless, or capable of making right decisions and gaining control of your thoughts and attitudes? How? Identify some examples

2. What areas of your life are most disciplined? In what areas do you lack discipline? Write out one example of each.

3. Identify one area that you can improve by working hard. How would you like to change in that area?

4. As pointed out in this chapter, we often do what we do because of poorly developed habits. What bad habits are holding you back from achieving authentic success? Make a list. Now, circle the most persistent one. How can you change this habit using the "take charge" principle?

Remember... *Take Charge!*

[i] Bill Gothard, *How to Conquer Slothfulness* (Institute of Basic Youth Conflicts: Oak Brook, IL, 1983).

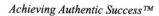

Become a Champion for Positive Impact!

2

Achieve Personal Significance

What You See...Is What You'll Be

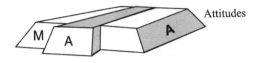

Attitudes

"The average person goes to his grave with his music still in him."
Oliver Wendell Holmes

Years ago, a teacher was assigned to the roughest class of boys in one of the toughest schools in Harlem, New York. One day she accidentally saw a listing of the boys' IQs and couldn't believe it. These guys were brilliant! So that's how she began treating them—as brilliant, capable human beings with incredible potential.

You can finish the story, can't you? They proved her right by graduating from high school and succeeding in great measure throughout their lives.

Yet here's the clincher: This teacher hadn't actually seen the boys' IQ scores. She had misread the paper; it was their locker numbers she had seen! Because she thought the numbers reflected their IQ scores and treated the boys as such, she dramatically changed the way they viewed *themselves*. If we see ourselves as people of significance—or if we think someone else believes we are smart—we'll act as if we are. But if we don't, we won't.

What you see is what you'll be. It's all a matter of your vision of yourself.

You are Significant!

Oliver Wendell Holmes said: "The biggest tragedy throughout the world is not the great waste of natural resources, though this is tragic. The greatest tragedy is the waste of human resources. The average person goes to his grave with his music still in him."

What about you? If you were to die today, would you go to the grave with your tune un-played? Are the instruments of your life—your talents, skills and abilities, relationships, the resources you've been given—starting to blend into beautiful music, or are they silent? Is the real you being stifled or held back? To recognize your significance, *you need to see that...*

1. You are Special...*Unique*

Maybe you've been called special by your parents all your life and now consider this to be a superficial compliment. Maybe you've never been singled out as special before. But you had better believe it, because it's absolutely true. You are the only *you* there will ever be, and regardless of how visible or invisible you feel, how popular or unpopular you think you are, how rich or poor you are, what your background is, *you are special.*

You've heard the phrase, "God don't make no junk." It's true. Consider for a few moments how important it is that you embrace your own specialness. *You aren't junk.* You exist to have a special impact on your world, in your area of influence.

You're the only one with your background, your contacts, and your personality. Therefore, there are many things in this life that only you are qualified to do. This is a reality you must fully embrace!

For some of us, our skills and abilities will touch thousands of other people. For others, our uniqueness will dramatically change the life of one or two other people during our lifetime. No matter who you touch, change, encourage or help, it is important to grasp that you have been created to do special and important things with your life.

Eleanor Roosevelt made an important statement when she said, "Nobody can make you feel inferior without your permission." How many times have you bought into someone else's opinion of you? How many times have you let their opinion become your reality?

You don't have to accept someone else's view that you are not important, that you don't have significance. You have been given a unique set of talents, skills and gifts. They were only given to you, and you have the opportunity to do whatever you want with them.

Hopefully, as you begin to accept the reality that you are special, you will recognize that you cannot only improve your own life, but also the lives of those around you. You will see yourself as a one-of-a-kind individual capable of limitless possibilities. This is how you were created.

2. You Can Make a Difference

There is only one you. You have been given a personality, personal skills, experiences (good and bad), inner drive and, most importantly, a mind to accomplish anything you really set your heart to. Whatever your thoughts are at this point it is crucial that you realize that what happened yesterday doesn't have to be what happens tomorrow. You see, today you have the opportunity to become the person you've always wanted to be: A person who…

- ➤ Exudes confidence
- ➤ Who shares his/her heart openly with others
- ➤ Who sees the potential for success in all areas

Not only will you gain psychological benefits by seeing yourself as an important, special person, you will also reap great social benefits as well. You will experience a new sense of confidence and energy.

But those aren't the only benefits. Think about how this attitude will affect your work. As your self-worth begins to grow, you'll see doors open that you've never noticed before. You'll have a sense of confidence that you never knew existed…confidence to go for the big jobs, important promotions and risky projects.

Those around you will benefit, too. Your confidence will become contagious. You'll spur others to do their best work and reach for their dreams, thus creating an atmosphere of success that will be hard to deny.

Once you recognize your significance, you must begin to identify your strengths. This will make you a much more effective leader, it will keep you from spending too much time in areas that you aren't particularly fond of, and it will cause you to be much more efficient with your time and energy. Maximizing your strengths can only lead you to achieve authentic success.

3. You Must Fulfill Your Destiny

When you realize and accept that one person (YOU!) alone can make a difference, you must believe that you can fulfill your destiny—that you can figure out and then live out what you are to do, and who you are to be at work, at home, and in your community. This is not optional. If you do not fulfill your destiny, unhappiness and a sense of failure will be your only companions. You have been placed on this earth for a reason.

You can begin to capture and define your destiny as you grow in your understanding of two major areas:

➢ Your *unique bents*

➢ Your *pressing needs* (those within your immediate sphere)

The more you understand these two areas the more precisely you can define your destiny. Your "bent" includes your gifts, abilities, opportunities, etc. Your "pressing needs" comprise those things that capture your heart, that require your involvement, including your own need to grow and develop.

Fundamentally, your destiny is being the BEST YOU you can be.

*Remember…*there is only one *you* with your gifts, skills and abilities. Combined with determination and a *make things happen* attitude, you will reach new levels of personal significance.

You Must Deal with Your Soft Spots (Weaknesses)

To establish significance, we must also deal with our soft spots, which we often choose to ignore. We all have soft spots (weaknesses), such as a bad temper, impatience, or a gossipy tongue. Contrary to popular practice, denying or hiding our weaknesses is not an effective way to deal with them. Also contrary to popular belief, these weaknesses are not that difficult to change.

Jim Collins, the popular management guru says, "the two keys to success in business today are intense professional will AND intense personal humility." Humility is critical to success in business productivity, profitability and overall growth.

1. Admit your Weaknesses

A popular book from some years ago by John Powell, *Why Am I Afraid to Tell You Who I Am?*, explained that people fear exposing themselves because they've concluded their friends and associates will not like what they see. People are afraid that their inner person —including their thoughts, attitudes, private behaviors, and vulnerabilities—would be rejected if truly understood by others.

Therefore, the author wrote, individuals develop masks to conceal who they are. The encouragement of the book was to learn to practice vulnerability. Take caution here. You shouldn't tell your deepest, darkest secrets to everyone. To do so would be unwise and inappropriate. However, appropriately sharing real needs to a small band of committed friends can be extremely helpful. Seeking insight and support is positive.

Moreover, having an open spirit to admit when you fail is attractive. It not only frees you to grow, but it provides an openness that can help others grow as well. Effective speakers and writers, who keep our attention and receive our admiration, speak and write with a degree of transparency before hundreds of people. They want to unlock the rigid, outer "performance" approach that people bring to life and success. That openness only makes their message more attractive to the rest of us. And it will be the same for you in your relationships. So, open up. Admit when you blow it!

2. Look for Opportunities to Grow

It's not enough merely to be open and admit your soft spots. You need to *actively* look for areas that need to change and ask for help in changing them. If you're not a part of an accountability group, you ought to be.

Find a group of friends in your business, neighborhood, church, or synagogue that will commit to helping you be more effective. Ask people to help who will encourage you, yet who will also be honest, loving, and caring enough to confront you and hold you accountable. It's a great way to grow.

For instance, share the following with several friends whom you trust: "Here are five questions I hope no one ever asks me." These five questions should represent the five weakest areas in your life. Such things as how you handle your finances, relational fidelity, your struggles with integrity, family difficulties, etc. The fifth question, then, is, "Did you lie about any of the above four?"

The contention is that if you're serious enough about growing you will not merely look for opportunities, but you will *create* the kind of situations that will help you grow. Practicing accountability is key to making the most of these opportunities.

3. Keep Adjusting

Finally, keep adjusting. Everyone makes mistakes. You will too, as you aim to improve your life. You will have days when you fail miserably, but that doesn't mean you can't do it. You are not a failure because you have some setbacks. Failing does not make you a failure. If you are continuing to learn from your mistakes and working hard not to repeat them, you can't help but succeed.

The important thing is that you keep trying and moving forward. Remember, the goal is not to become perfect, because none of us can be perfect in this life. The goal is to progress, to move forward and to begin the transformation into authentically successful living. That will happen as you achieve the personal significance that embodies all of your gifts and talents and deals with your weaknesses and soft spots.

The key is to keep learning, admitting mistakes and moving on.

Too often we approach life like Garfield the comic strip cat. Garfield says, "I didn't do it! I didn't do it! I didn't do it! I didn't do it!" He slyly admits, "Rehearsing." Then you see the question coming from outside the frame: "All right! Who glued Odie to the ceiling?" And Garfield is ready for his act. "Showtime!" he gloats.

In pretending to be perfect, we, too, take up that mantra: "I didn't do it! It wasn't my fault! I didn't make a mistake." In our refusal to admit our mistakes, to appear imperfect, we actually lie! We forget, or we don't accept, that we're not here to perform but to progress, and progression involves admitting mistakes and moving on from them.

Admittedly, it's difficult dealing with criticism, but we *need* it! It's possible to embrace criticism and learn to use it and not overreact to it. Remember, it's better to have constructive criticism from a friend than empty praise or manipulative flattery from an enemy. A lot of us get deluded with faulty praise and flattery. It does us no good to have an untrue perception of ourselves. The purpose of our lives is progress, not a pretense to perfection.

Don't pretend to be perfect...
but progress in authentic success.

Lewis Timberlake tells a great story about achieving personal significance.

Nestled back in the hills lay a small cabin inhabited by a carpenter and his barely literate wife. They could scarcely eke out a living from carpentry work and wood chopping which were their only means of support. So when a son was born to them it was only natural that the father would eventually train him in carpentry and wood chopping as well.

This tall, lanky boy chopped wood for his father until he was twenty-one. But chopping wood wouldn't satisfy his hunger for knowledge. So he borrowed books and read by candlelight during the evening hours. The things he learned in those books planted dreams in his mind of better things, of other occupations, and of other worlds beyond his little country town.

At the age of twenty-three he ran as a candidate for his state's legislature and lost. He continued to study during his spare time, his thirst for knowledge unquenchable. His dream was to become a lawyer and after studying alone for many years he finally passed his bar exam at age twenty-seven. By then he had worked on a Mississippi ferryboat, in a mill, a general store and post office, as a farmhand and as a surveyor and had served in his state's militia.

He found a partner, went into practice and went bankrupt. All of this happened in a relatively short period of time. He spent the next sixteen years of his life paying off the debts his firm had incurred.

He fell in love with a beautiful young lady who broke their engagement and his heart as well. She later died.

At the age of thirty-three he finally married a young woman with a strong will and a temper to match. Their marriage proved to be as stormy and volatile as her temper. Of the four sons born to them, three died before reaching adulthood.

At age thirty-five he reopened his law practice. His desire to serve in public office proved as insatiable as his quest for knowledge. Even though he had lost one election twelve years earlier he optimistically sought office again and lost again. At age forty-seven his party selected him as their vice presidential candidate. Again he lost. At forty-nine he was nominated for the United States Senate and again lost.

Here was a man whose formal schooling at age twenty-two totaled less than one year. He lost the love of his life, his law practice and three sons. He had a rocky and stormy marriage. He sought public office numerous times only to be defeated time and time again. By anyone's definition of a failure, this man must certainly have been one.

However, in spite of all these failures he did experience a few successes. At age twenty-five after having lost a bid for the state legislature he came back and won, serving four terms. At age thirty-eight after losing a bid for a congressional seat three years earlier, he was elected to congress for one term. After losing the vice presidential nomination and a U.S. Senate seat he was nominated as the Republican Party's presidential candidate at age fifty-one and won. At age fifty-five he was re-nominated and reelected to a second presidential term. His name was Abraham Lincoln.

History has testified that Abraham Lincoln not only emancipated the slaves but he also became a strong party leader who maintained a faith in democracy that rubbed off on his countrymen and people all over the world. He became an international symbol of man's quest for freedom. After many failures he remained undaunted, coming back and changing the course of history.

Achieving personal significance is a vital component in achieving authentic success. As you move toward living a successful life remember that you are special. You have gifts and talents to offer the world around you. Find your personal significance by helping others, striving for your goals and surrounding yourself with people who respect you and challenge you to grow.

Remember, no one can make you feel inferior without your permission. Now go out and live the life you were put on earth to live—a life of purpose, meaning, joy and personal significance.

Action Steps

1. Take some time to fill in the following statements. Try to add three specifics for each one.
    - ➢ I am special because…
    - ➢ I can make a difference in these ways…
    - ➢ I have been put here on earth to…

2. A few major soft spots I need to admit to others and myself are…

3. Here's how I will look for opportunities to grow this year…

MAXIMIZERS CREED

M	I will take charge of my life and make a difference.
A	I will live my life with a sense of dignity.
X	I will embrace problems as positive opportunities.
I	I will center my life on universal principles.
M	I will passionately pursue my mission.
I	I will keep all vital areas of my life in balance.
Z	I will put others first and honestly serve them.
E	I will cultivate my character and spirit.
R	I will keep adjusting to needs.
S	I will never, ever, ever quit.

Be A Critical Thinker...
With A Positive Attitude!

3

X-out the Negatives

Don't Say Why, Say What

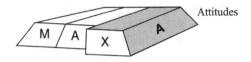

"Our doubts are traitors and make us lose the good we oft might win by fearing to attempt."

Shakespeare

Justifying our actions seems to be a universally human defense mechanism. Do you find this sort of thing happening with companies you do business with, or among your own managers and employees?

Think about it. For instance, the following are actual explanations made on insurance forms by people who were in car accidents:

- The guy was all over the road. I had to swerve a number of times before I finally hit him.

- I pulled away from the side of the road, glanced at my *mother-in-law,* and went over the embankment.

- I'd been driving my car for forty years when I fell asleep at the wheel and had an accident.

- The pedestrian had no idea which direction to run so I ran over him.

- The telephone pole was approaching fast. I was attempting to swerve out of its path when it struck my front end.

What we call rationalization is often our choice to view things from an untrue perspective—particularly a perspective that might make us look good rather than reveal the ugly truth.

In this chapter I want to deal with perspective and attitude. It's the "X" in our MAXIMIZERS model, and I call this approach *X-out the negatives*.

The name of the game in dealing with life's problems is not to ask why bad things happen to us. Instead, we should ask, what can I learn from this? How can I use this challenge to grow? It's all a matter of attitude and perspective, of focusing not on the difficulty but on what lessons we can gain from it.

The Chinese have a saying: "Crisis creates opportunity."

We need to focus on our opportunities.

The key to putting this principle into practice is your *perspective*, that is, how you look at things. Stephen Covey, one of the wisest business counselors and educators today, tells an interesting story of how his own view changed. As he sat on a commuter train one night, he noticed a father sitting in the corner while his children played in front of him. Apparently the children got louder and louder, and more obnoxious, but the father didn't do anything about it.

It was obvious to Covey and others nearby that the situation was getting out of control. Finally, in desperation, Covey went to the father and said, "Those are pretty active children, aren't they?"

The father turned to him and said,

"I guess so. Frankly, I hadn't noticed. We just came from the hospital where their mother died." At that moment Covey's perspective changed. He had seen something one way in one moment and another way the next.

Martin Seligman in his book, *Learned Optimism,* developed a test called the Attribution Style Questionnaire (ASQ) to compare pessimism and optimism. In this test, subjects are asked to concoct a story explaining the cause of good and bad events in a series of situations. The higher the ASQ score the greater the likelihood that the person taking the test has a pessimistic attitude.

The ASQ was used with American swimmers who were training for the 1980 Seoul Olympics. After the swimmers took the test, their coaches decided to play a trick on them, adding seconds to the swimmers' real lap times during a practice session. When the swimmers were given these wrong times, they were told to rest and then swim again.

The performance of those who were pessimists deteriorated on the second attempt by two seconds. They believed the bad news. The optimists kept a steady pace, and a few, including Matt Biondi, swam even faster. Matt went on to win five gold medals in those Olympic Games.[i]

Pessimism can be detrimental at the least, and deadly at most. Think of the productivity that is lost by employees who possess pessimistic attitudes. Not only are their tasks done less confidently, but also many innovations never take place because of their negative mind-set. Moreover, the toll on relationships that comes out of pessimism and negative attitudes is enormous.

Negativism can be a major roadblock on the path to success. A negative attitude or outlook takes a vast amount of energy to keep up. It keeps you from using that energy to foster change, encourage others and move in a forward direction.

For many people a negative outlook on life is a form of protection. When we have been hurt or when our self-esteem is low we try to find some way to keep people from seeing the real person inside. We use our attitude to hold people at arms' length. We don't want to feel any more pain, so we cut them off with hurtful words and sometimes, hurtful actions.

Living this way is hard. If you have spent any time around someone whose outlook is always pessimistic then you understand. Negativism takes a toll on everyone. But viewing the world from a negative perspective isn't the only way to protect yourself.

When you decide that you want to make a difference in the world around you and you embrace your uniqueness, truly believing that you are special, then you are already on the road to success. You are traveling on a path of living that only you can control. You are empowered to go in bold new directions.

Add to that a positive outlook on life and you become a winner almost by default. You can't help but see goodness, light and life. If you make the choice to have a negative outlook, however, then you become a *loser* by default. The world becomes a dark and daunting place and there is little or no impetus to move forward or make a difference.

I want to focus on three areas I call the ABCs of right attitudes. These are the life tools needed to "X out the negatives" in your life.

➢ *A* is *accept* problems; don't deny them.

➢ *B* is *believe* the best.

➢ *C* is *cast off* the negatives.

Accept Problems

Don't deny problems. It's a simple reality that life is difficult. What you make of your life depends on the challenges you choose to accept or seek. Small house…small problems; big house… big problems.

Garfield, the author of the outstanding work, *Peak Performers* states, "winners see and embrace problems but they look at them as challenges, opportunities, strategic options and seldom even use the word problem. This makes their handling of these issues responsive and positive, not reactive and negative."

Ultimately, you make the choice. Do you want a satisfying, challenging life, or do you want to sit back and accept an unsatisfying life? Do you want to be significant or insignificant? Your significance will be measured in direct proportion to your response to the difficulties you face.

1. Learn From Your Mistakes

Think of the three worst failures in your life. What are they? Maybe one was a marriage that fell apart. Maybe another was becoming trapped in alcoholism. Maybe you failed miserably at a job. Ask the following questions about the failures in your life:

✓ What did you learn from these mistakes?

✓ Where did they lead you?

In Mary Craig's words: "The only cure for suffering is to face it head on, grasp it around the neck, and use it. Looking back, it is clear to see how I needed those failed experiences for the things I am doing today. In a sense, I didn't fail because I learned from experience. As Sophocles the playwright once said, 'There is no success without hardship.'"

2. Choose Joy

In the pursuit of authentic success problems *do* arise and it is in these times that you have to consciously choose to be joyful. In the midst of struggles and hardships choosing to be cheerful and optimistic may mean the difference between a difficult learning experience and disappointing failure.

Do you feel joyful today? Are you aware that deep down no matter what happens you will make it through? Do you have a sustaining sense of peace that buoys your life? Joy is a choice.

3. Take Risks

Everyone starts out with the best of intentions. We want to be successful, happy, make right choices and set a good example. Many times we fall off the track. We make poor choices or someone around us makes a wrong choice that affects us. We get bogged down in the details of life and lose sight of what is important.

Taking risks keeps us on our toes. We have to make prudent decisions, smart choices and take leaps of faith to really live full and productive lives. Our experiences push us to new levels and create numerous opportunities for each of us to grow.

Many times life throws us curve balls. We try to plan everything and yet things rarely turn out the way we expect. But as the great Babe Ruth said, "Never let the fear of striking out get in your way." It is being willing to expect the unexpected that creates a life that is authentically successful. Joseph Campbell said it well.

"We must be willing to get rid of the life we've planned,
so as to have the life that is waiting for us."

We don't know what life has in store for us. We can't see the future in a crystal ball, but we can be prepared to take risks and remain optimistic in spite of hurdles that are thrown into our path.

Believe The Best

As we think, so we act. Therefore, you must take control of your thought patterns by believing the best about the following areas: yourself, life and other people. The key to having the right view toward each of these areas is to use the right methodology to support and cultivate this view.

1. Right View Toward Self: Affirming

When you want to think the best about yourself, practice the art of affirming. Affirm yourself. The way to do this is to apply what I said in Chapter 2 about achieving personal significance. On the one hand you're to say, "I'm significant." On the other you're to say, "I have soft spots." You have to constantly balance both of these truths.

One does not exist without the other. You're significant, and you have soft spots that need midcourse correction. And you affirm yourself by believing both of these aspects of your humanness. When you keep them before you daily and live in light of them, you can know you're doing all you can.

2. Right View Toward Life: Thanking

Establish the right view toward life. A key word here is *thankfulness*. Someone said, "Instead of living in the present tense, we need to live in the pleasant tense." We need to go about life living it to the fullest with a sense of gratitude.

Frederick Buechner suggests that key to living life to the fullest is measuring how fully we experience it day in and day out. Buechner asks: "Have you wept at anything during the past year? Have you thought seriously about the fact that someday you're going to die?

More often than not, do you really listen when people are speaking to you instead of just waiting for your turn to speak? Is there anybody you know, to whom if one of you had to suffer great pain, you would volunteer yourself?"

His point is that living life to the fullest requires deep involvement. Thanksgiving arises from the poignancy of life around us, from a full awareness of the gift we've been given to care for others, to enjoy nature, to give ourselves away, etc.

We must live with an expressed thanksgiving to whatever form God takes in our mind. We must say, "Thank you, God, for my life and my health. Thank you for my opportunities. And thank you for my problems." The way to develop a right perspective and believe the best about life is by constantly being thankful. *It's the attitude of gratitude.*

I recall coaching a group of executives in a Fortune 400 construction company about this concept of thankfulness. This was pretty counter-intuitive for them because these very sharp men and women were pros at finding problems and creating zero defect work environments. I only spent about 10 minutes addressing this as part of a larger set of skills.

Three months later my associate and I came back for another coaching session and we asked the leaders how their lives had changed while we were gone. We also added the following: "We are here to help you get your lives straight, whole, productive and profitable. If it isn't working, you need to fire us because we are costly and, frankly, you're wasting our time."

Immediately, one of the 29-year-old GenXer's raised his hand and said,

"Dr. Jenson, since you were here last my whole life has changed." I responded, "Really!! How?"

He went on to explain that prior to the previous session he got up every morning and worried about the 15 things he had to have done by noon. He said he was rude to his wife, dismissed his two small children, was offensive to his co-workers and sub-contractors and, on a personal level, he was miserable and tied up in knots.

But, he went on to say,

"I've taken your advice and have made it a habit to get up every morning and be thankful for my wife, my children, my life, the blue sky, my great job and company and even my challenges. And, everyone is seeing the difference. AND, I am so much more satisfied, productive and profitable."

I turned to the rest of the team and said, "Is this accurate?" And they all agreed heartily.

Then, this young Yale graduate said something that almost made me fall out of my chair. "Dr. Jenson, no one ever before told me that I should be thankful." What a tragedy!!

Well, I don't want to make the same mistake with *you*. May I be the first to say, *be thankful*. Have the attitude of gratitude and watch your personal and professional life become transformed.

3. Right View Toward People: Building Up

The key to believing the best about people is to have the building up of others as your *modus operandi*. When you think of people, think of building up. When you're talking to or about people, use words that build up, not ones that tear down. We develop this concept more and give you some methods in Chapter 7 that deals with *Zeroing in on Caring for People*.

Cast Off the Negative

Now that you've changed your attitude about yourself, about life and about others, let's turn to another way of dealing with attitudes: learn to

(1) Reject your fears

(2) Root out doubts

(3) Realize your possibilities

Perhaps you're in a situation in which you need to address some difficulties. Certainly the support of a group and wise counsel can help. But ultimately, you must take responsibility and begin to focus your thoughts on the positive. Remember that your emotions flow out of the way you perceive life.

1. Reject Your Fears

I've learned through my research in education programs over the years that even though I can help people accept problems and truly embrace them, those same people can be completely immobilized by the negatives they allow to rule their lives.

Zig Ziglar says, "Fear is the darkroom where negatives are developed." Sometimes our fears are quite profound, complicated and deep. At other times, they are very simple.

The first step to overcoming your fears is confronting them. Allowing yourself to remember and identify past things that cause you to be fearful can completely paralyze you and keep you from growing and developing in the present and future. But you can learn to reject your fears by attaching new meaning to your experiences.

First, *identify your fear*… write it down (start with something easy).

Second, *visualize your fear* and begin to attach something pleasurable to your fear, versus something painful.

Third, *confront your fear* head on. Do something positive around your identified fear that causes you to begin pushing out this rooted fear in your life.

Fourth, *celebrate your success* (large or small).

Fifth, *identify another* paralyzing fear that is holding you back and challenge yourself to conquer it by repeating the above steps. Until you learn to reject your fears, you can be inhibited from being all that you can be.

2. Root Out Doubts

You now need to deal with your doubts. We all have doubts; no one is free of them. Much of energetic and positive living is making the decision *not* to doubt, and instead to think optimistically about even the difficult things in our lives.

We can learn a lot in this regard from the cognitive therapy field. The basis of cognitive therapy is that we have emotional problems because we think wrongly. The key to positive emotions, once again, is positive, accurate thinking—having the right image of oneself and thinking right. Dr. David Burns, in his classic book, *Feeling Good,* explains the impact of this thinking. He writes that what happens in our minds are cognitive (thinking) distortions.

There are multiple cognitive distortions. One distortion is called "all or nothing" thinking. In this mind-set, an individual sees everything in black-and-white categories. If his performance falls short of perfect, he sees himself as a total failure.

Another distortion is over generalization. This is when a single, negative event is seen as a never-ending pattern of defeat.

Another is disqualifying the positive. Here you reject positive experiences by insisting they don't count for some reason or another. A person with such distortions can maintain a negative belief that is contradicted by his everyday experiences.

Dealing with your doubts begins by thinking accurately about a situation. If you doubt you can do something, articulate in your mind the reasons why you can't do it, and then write down plausible reasons why you think you *can* do it.[ii]

3. Realize Your Possibilities

In the 1952 Olympics, a young Hungarian boy peered down the barrel of his gun and hit the bull's-eye repeatedly. He was flawless. His perfect hand and eye coordination had won him the gold medal. Tragically, he lost his right arm, his shooting arm, six months later. But just four years after this he went to the Olympic Games in Melbourne, where he won his second gold medal with his *left* hand. He had determined not to be restricted by his limitations but, instead, to see his possibilities.

Tim Hansel says, "Limitations are not necessarily negative.

In fact, I'm beginning to believe that they can give life definition, clarity, and freedom. We are called to freedom of and in limitations—not from. Unrestricted water is swamp; because it lacks restriction, it also lacks depth."

If you want depth—if you want power, real freedom, and clarity—you need to learn to live with your limitations and to embrace them. And if you're going to maximize your life you need to learn to *X out the negatives* and live with the belief that you can do whatever you want in life.

As you begin to master this life skill, as well as the two other attitudinal life skills (making things happen and achieving personal significance), you will have the foundation needed to move on to your belief principles.

Action Steps

1. Think of a major problem in your life right now? How are you handling it? Write down your feelings, thoughts, and previous actions related to this problem.

2. Choose joy. Write down how you will respond as you embrace the above problem as a friend, rather than treating it as an intruder. Be specific about what you will think, feel, and act. Then practice this process repeatedly until it becomes a habit.

3. Choose an area in which you should believe the best (yourself, life, problems, people). Incorporate into your life the methods recommended in this chapter. They will change your attitude. Again, write down specifically how you will think, feel, and act, and practice these until they become an instinctive part of you.

4. Choose a person in your life to whom you can be accountable to practice the above changes for one month. Choose someone who will encourage you and build you up as you attempt to grow and move forward.

---

[i] Martin Seligman, *Learned Optimism* (New York: Random House, 1991).

[ii] David Burns, *Feeling Good* (New York: Signet Books, 1980).

You must identify and promote the values you want to characterize yourself. Or, you can expect to spend the rest of your life as a slave to other people's values, your own dysfunctions, cultural pressures, or the values your own bad habits produce. The choice is yours!

Section 2

Root Beliefs

H ave you ever wondered why you do what you do—why you lose your temper, eat unhealthy food, spend money impulsively or engage in activities that just waste your time?

We believe we do these things because we have become slaves to the world around us–to our backgrounds, our friends and associates, the media, and other purveyors of the culture's values. The problem is: those values may not be *your* values.

The only way to change this trend and move toward the maximization of your life and profession is to plant and deepen *belief roots*. And the two major principles that you need to frame the direction of your life makes up the next two chapters: *Internalize Right Principles* and *March to a Mission*.

Internalize Right Principles deals with the development of a personal, principle-based value system. Either you must develop your own clearly defined values rooted in right principles, or you will continue to be led by the culture. In this chapter, we explain how to identify and build right values into your life. These right values must form the foundation to your life and empower you to practice what we call *rightness living*. The fulfillment and satisfaction you experience as you begin to align your time and resources around your values will be one of the greatest journeys of your life.

March to a Mission will further help you frame your life and activities around a deliberate, well-thought-out sense of mission. In this chapter, we offer specific steps for you to follow as you articulate your purpose and mission in life. And we help you work through your beliefs about the major roles you have and specific goals you want to achieve.

These two belief principles will give you the framework, confidence, and power to achieve authentic success in your personal and professional life.

What are the principles that guide your personal and business life? Learn to be transformed by the renewing of your mind!

4

Internalize Right Principles

How to Do the Right Thing

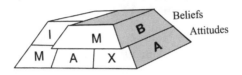

"You never know a line is crooked unless you have a straight one to put next to it."

Socrates

Establishing right principles in our hearts and minds so they affect our decision making is the focus of this fourth principle from the MAXIMIZERS acrostic—*internalize right principles.*

Consider what columnist Jack Griffin says in his little piece called "It's OK, Son, Everybody Does It," printed in the Chicago Sun Times:

> When Johnny was 6 years old, he was with his father when they were caught speeding. His father handed the officer a twenty-dollar bill with his driver's license. "It's OK, son," his father said as they drove off. "Everybody does it."

> When he was 8, he was present at a family council presided over by Uncle George, on the surest means to shave points off the income tax return. "It's OK, kid," his uncle said. "Everybody does it."

> When he was 9, his mother took him to his first theater production. The box office man couldn't find any seats until his mother discovered an extra $5 in her purse. "It's OK, son," she said. "Everybody does it."

When he was 12, he broke his glasses on the way to school. His Aunt Francine persuaded the insurance company that they had been stolen and they collected $75. "It's OK, kid," she said. "Everybody does it."

When he was 15, he made right guard on the high school football team. His coach showed him how to block and at the same time grab the opposing end by the shirt so the official couldn't see it. "It's OK, kid," the coach said. "Everybody does it."

When he was 16, he took his first summer job at the supermarket. His assignment was to put the overripe strawberries in the bottom of the boxes and the good ones on top where they would show. "It's OK, kid," the manager said. "Everybody does it."

When he was 18, Johnny and a neighbor applied for a college scholarship. Johnny was a marginal student. His neighbor was in the upper 3 percent of his class, but he couldn't play right guard. Johnny got the scholarship. "It's OK, son," his parents said. "Everybody does it."

When he was 19, he was approached by an upperclassman that offered the test answers for $50. "It's OK, kid," he said. "Everybody does it."

Johnny was caught and sent home in disgrace. "How could you do this to your mother and me?" his father said. "You never learned anything like this at home." His aunt and uncle were also shocked.

If there's one thing the adult world can't stand, it's a kid who cheats....[i]

Correlate that story with this article written by syndicated columnist Cal Thomas:

It was anything but coincidental when just five weeks before the Stock Market crisis *The Wall Street Journal* carried this story in its September 8, 1987 edition with the headline: "Ethics Are Nice, But They Can Be A Handicap, Some Executives Declare."

The story reported on a survey conducted by the research firm McFeely Wackerle Jett. It asked 671 managers their views on the subject of ethics and business. The managers contended that ethics can impede a successful career and that more than half the executives they know would bend the rules to get ahead.

"I know of unethical acts at all levels of management," one fifty-year-old executive quoted in the study said. As his rationale for being unethical at times, he said, "I have to do it in order to survive."

For him, survival became the end, not honesty or truth. When such thinking becomes dominant in a culture, that culture is doomed.

The McFeely study also found that older executives generally think they are more principled than their younger counterparts. This is easily understandable given the sociological and moral upheaval younger men and women have gone through during the past twenty-five years.

The study quoted a fifty-nine-year-old vice-president at a Midwest company as saying, "Young M.B.A.'s and lawyers are taught opportunism, cleverness and cunning. Fairness and equity aren't given equal time or importance."[ii]

Compare what was happening in 1987 to what is happening **today**. The headlines are clear—honesty, ethics, virtue, integrity and straight-lines, as Socrates calls them, have eroded and the entire culture demonstrates this devastation.

This needs to change! And, it needs to begin with you. Stability and strength, and consequently success and significance, flow out of absolute values—characteristics like honesty and integrity.

Remember, *YOU impact others with the way you handle your values.*

So, let me coach you in a process that will help you identify and begin building absolute values on the subject of morals and ethics.

Here's another acrostic that will focus your thinking:

V erify your own values

A rticulate your own ethical grid and philosophy of life

L earn the proper perspectives on issues

U npack right values through action

E valuate your growth

S hare these truths (your principles) with other people

Verify Your Own Values

You need to determine just what values are directing your life. It's important from the outset to distinguish between principles and values. Basically, a value is your perception of where you're going in life. It's changeable. A principle is absolute. Principles are always true in every circumstance, while values may change as understanding increases. These principles are the roots that are cultivated by the nutrient soil of truth (absolute truth). Values may or may not be rooted in absolute truth.

Everyone is value-driven. A gang member is directed by his or her values. So are a mass murderer, a priest and a dockworker. Everyone you know has values. The question is this…

> Are their values, are *your* values, based on right or wrong universal principles?

Right universal principles produce healthy roots of authentic success. Wrong universal principles ultimately produce failure.

What is it that you value?

When this question is asked of people attending seminars, they usually try to articulate what they think they *should* value. But that's not the question! You should identify what you value *right now*. What values are reflective of your present lifestyle? Be honest! A rather rigorous evaluation here is critical; otherwise, you will miss the opportunity to identify the real root areas in your life that may need to change.

You can't expect an empty bag to stand up straight!

If we don't have ethics or principles to give us substance and weight—if we're empty in the things that matter—we won't be the kind of role models we want and need to be. Change begins with our value systems. And if the values of our *society* are declining, it's our fault.

Try this exercise:

Conduct a one-week, authentic audit of your life by answering these questions every day:

> ➢ How do you spend your discretionary time?

> ➢ How do you spend your discretionary money?

> ➢ Who are your heroes?

> ➢ When you're alone, what do you think about most?

Keep a daily log, and stop several times throughout the day to record your observations. Be honest and record what you are and do *now*, not what you *think* you ought to be and do. That will come later.

Then, at the end of the week, go back and determine the things that you actually valued during that week. Your answers will demonstrate what your values are. Next, ask yourself whether these are the values you want. Are you using your time, spending your money, focusing your dreams, and developing your role models the way you want to?

Articulate Your Universal Principles

What is really important to you? Some people believe that the ethical thing to do is always "whatever will get me ahead." Take time right now to identify the things that are non-negotiable in your life—principles you will not violate, no matter what. Include principles that affect your work, your personal life, your family, your finances, and your spirituality.

What is your personal philosophy or code of ethics? What is your family philosophy? What is your work philosophy?

Begin your self-examination with the ten MAXIMIZERS principles set forth in this book. The ultimate goal is to dig your roots down to the bedrock of *truth* and let that source frame your values. If you do not articulate these values, if you do not settle your mind on what is right and wrong, the culture will continually push you around. You must identify and promote the values you want to characterize yourself, values based on universal principles. If not, you can expect to spend the rest of your life as a slave to other's values, your own dysfunctions, cultural pressures, or the values your own bad habits produce. The choice is yours.

Learn the Right Perspective on Issues

Merely discovering what motivates your actions is not the end of this exercise. All of us need to continually look for *truth* and then to apply it to our lives.

Where do we find truth? Where do we get the raw material that helps form our values? We study history and cultures—in other words, we study life. Read the classic books that have impacted society year after year. Discuss what you read with a small group. Hunt for effective creeds that have directed others in the past, from the Boy Scout Oath to the Ten Commandments, to mention only two.

Despite what many say, there *are* absolutes—universally accepted natural law principles that govern the universe and how people should live. Daily, we need to make actual determinations about right and wrong, about the ethical and unethical, about the moral, amoral, and immoral.

In *The Power of Ethical Management*, Ken Blanchard and Dr. Norman Vincent Peale simplify decision-making with three questions to ask yourself. I've added a fourth:

1. Is it legal? (Will I be violating either civil law or company policy?)

2. Is it balanced? (Is it fair to all concerned in the short-term as well as the long-term? Does it promote a win-win situation?)

3. How will it make me feel about myself? (Will it make me proud? Would I feel good if my decision were published in the newspaper, or if my family knew about it?)

4. Is it right? (Do I have any concerns inside as I consider my decision in light of what I understand to be right and wrong?)

Unpack Right Values Through Action

Now you're ready to start putting your values to work. It's one thing to develop an ethical grid of universal principles (truth) but quite another to work it out in your daily life.

For example, here's a strategy for treating the various people in your life the right way by using the MAXIMIZERS principle *zero in on caring for people.*

First, recognize that the underlying approach you need with everyone is a sense of personal humility. Jim Collins, in his breakthrough Harvard work, *From Good to Great,* identifies humility as one of the two core qualities of a "level 5 leader."

This is most popularly called "servant leadership." It is a code that urges you to build up other people in all possible ways. In the mid-1970s John Greenleaf, former director of management research at AT&T, wrote a landmark book entitled *Servant Leadership.*

Servant leadership, as Greenleaf describes it, focuses on your responsibility to build others, rather than on your rights and perks from being in a leadership position. It is this kind of leadership that says, "I'm here to care for people and help them become successful." To live by this principle, you have to *burn this value of servant leadership into your mind.* You can do this by writing down a popular quotation or statement on servant leadership. For instance, *"A servant leader is one who gets excited about making others more successful than himself."*

Put these words on a 3x5-inch card and keep it before you during the day. Meditate on it at least four times. Think it through; chew on it; eat it up. Focus on that card as soon as you get up in the morning. Take a break at lunch and think about it. Reflect on it before dinner and then later, just before you go to sleep. Program your mind with this thought.

Next, think about ways you can apply this principle. Ask yourself questions about how you can be a servant leader in your personal and professional life. With whom do you have regular contact? Perhaps it's a gas station attendant, a waitress, or people you call on the phone. Perhaps it's your boss or a fellow employee. Include your spouse and children. Your friends. How can you be a source of encouragement to these people?

Think through various situations that will come up in your daily activities and plan your servant-leadership attack before they happen. You're bound to meet a grumpy waiter or waitress every now and then. What will you do? In the arena of your family, your servant leadership may mean taking very deliberate time to be with your children, perhaps developing dates on a regular basis. These need to be planned, thought out, and activated. In the arena of your business, your servant leadership might be seen in the way you develop your employees or those for whom you have responsibility.

Evaluate Your Growth

To become truly ethically centered, spend time evaluating your efforts on a daily basis. Keep a journal of your growth for one week, taking time at the end of each day to ask the following questions related to your stated values:

➤ Did I schedule my principles and values into my daily planner?

➤ Did I keep my schedule as I planned?

➤ How did I spend my idle time?

➤ Where did I spend my money?

➤ What did I daydream or dwell upon?

➤ Did my values inside match my values outside?

Establish a support group whose members will ask you regularly how you're doing. One reason Weight Watchers and Jenny Craig are such effective weight-loss organizations is the accountability that personal trainers or coaches provide. However you choose to motivate yourself, the impact of accountability and support works very well.

Share These Truths with Others

I believe we ought to be sharing values in our culture. In fact, I believe we ought to be *champions* of right values and principles. We can do this by being both *formative* and *reformative* in our communications.

Being *formative* means trying to construct truth in people's lives by talking about and modeling right principles. For example, I have put my ten MAXIMIZERS principles on my business card in an effort to put values at the forefront of people's thinking. Many principle-centered people I know display plaques on their office walls or desks with well-chosen sayings that communicate values, such as the leadership quote I shared earlier.

The second way you can build these qualities into people's lives is by being *reformative*, taking the initiative to challenge others' behavior, getting them to examine their own values.

There are right ways and wrong ways to do this. First, communicate *personally*. Be brave and be direct in your personal interaction.

Second, communicate *positively*. It doesn't help to say to someone, "Here are twenty-five things you're doing wrong, and I only want to deal with one of them at this point." Instead, say, "There are many things in your life I wish I had in mine, but here's something I believe you may want to work on."

Third, communicate *practically*. There's nothing worse than identifying a generic problem with someone's thinking or behavior and not give that person specific examples to change and new thoughts to consider.

Finally, communicate *patiently*. Lack of patience damages our credibility and therefore our impact. Significant values shifts take time.

Whether you communicate with reformative or formative activity, you must aim to be a champion for values. Be a servant leader. Don't include yourself in the majority who are afraid to talk about truth, either because they haven't come to any conclusions or are afraid of repercussions.

Don't leave a legacy of relativity behind you. Leave a legacy of values, of truth, of rightness. It's your choice.

Once you have committed to building bedrock, universal principles and embedding the roots of these principles into truth, into your life, then you are ready to move on to the next belief principle: *March to a Mission.*

Action Steps

Values Clarification Exercise

➢ Where do you spend your discretionary time?

➢ How do you spend your discretionary money?

➢ Who are your heroes?

➢ When you're all alone, what do you think about the most?

➢ What do the answers to these questions tell you about your values? Are they the same values you thought you lived by?

Principle Development

1. What are the principles with which you want to form the map for your life? Begin to write these down. Place them prominently before you and begin to build them into your life as your code of conduct and organizing principles.

2. List at least one other person who can form a support group to help you flesh out your values and walk your talk.

---

[i] Jack Griffin quoted in Ken Blanchard and Norman Peale, *The Power of Ethical Management* (New York: William Morrow and Company, 1988), pg. 30-31.

[ii] Cal Thomas, *The Death of Ethics in America* (Waco, TX: Word, 1988), pg. 50-51.

5
March to a Mission

Beyond Success to Significance

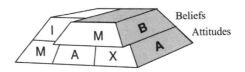

"This is the true joy in life...the being thoroughly worn out before you are thrown on the scrap heap; the being a force of Nature instead of a feverish, selfish little clod of ailments..."

George Bernard Shaw

We all have rules for our lives. We arrive at some values through thoughtful processes; other values are passed down to us from our parents; still others we develop from we-don't-know-where. Suffice it to say we all live by guideposts—certain principles that form the grid through which we see and do things.

The fifth principle in the MAXIMIZERS model is the phrase *march to a mission*. It addresses the area of establishing guideposts for our lives. This chapter is about focusing on the present—not avoiding the past or ignoring the future, but rather marshaling your energies toward that part of life over which you have control. This is the opportunity of a lifetime—to change your life by establishing a framework for success.

"March to a mission" means living with a sense of destiny, passion, excitement and meaning. It means knowing that you are living your life in a significant way. There are so many distractions in today's world that can shift your attention.

It is vital that you have a firmly established aim to guide you through each day. Failing to set your sights on a goal or refusing to march to your mission can easily keep you from achieving the success you desire.

If you are a manger or business owner, take a moment to think about some of your employees. What sets the really good workers apart from the rest? Most likely you notice their work habits and get a sense about what drives them. A good employee usually has a goal or mission they are striving after that motivates them to work well. A bad employee is usually aimless, disengaged and lacks direction.

Think about how much you could improve the efficiency of your company or department by helping others to find their mission. What a difference a little guidance can make for anyone, from the CEO to the mailroom clerk.

The Power of a Mission

A sense of mission gives *meaning and significance to our lives*. Nietzsche said, "If a man has a *why* to live for, he can stand any *how*." In other words, if someone has a sense of purpose, he can endure all the problems he faces in getting to his goal.

David Rae has conducted research among his peers in the Young Presidents Organization, discovering that most CEOs are less afraid of dying than they are of not making a contribution to their world. Indeed, Harold Kushner says, "I believe that it is not dying that people are afraid of. Something else. Something more unsettling and more tragic than dying frightens us. We're afraid of never having lived. We are afraid of coming to the end of our days with the sense that we were never really alive. That we never figured out what life was for."

Viktor Frankl said, "More and more people today have the means to live but no meaning to live for." As you develop mission in life, you also develop a *mooring*—something that anchors you and results in stability. This mooring helps you to see things with greater clarity, which in turn results in inner strength, meaning and significance.

To help you gain mooring and stability, we suggest you develop a mission statement for your life. A mission statement will serve as a beacon, guiding you for the rest of your life in the right direction. Whatever you do from that point on will be anchored in the principles and values you hold precious.

A sense of mission also helps you develop greater *motivation*. A mission serves as a *source for starting and sustaining* a project. Without it, people get stuck going around and around in circles, captive to their habits, unable to motivate themselves to make a fresh start on important things.

Mission takes us away from an endless cycle of existence. It creates a motivation for us to move ahead with purpose and direction. It gives us a sense of destiny. It gives us a reason for getting out of bed in the morning.

We need to live with the spirit behind the challenging words of George Bernard Shaw: "This is the true joy in life, the being used for a purpose recognized by yourself as a mighty one; the being thoroughly worn out before you are thrown on the scrap heap; the being a force of Nature instead of a feverish selfish little clod of ailments and grievances complaining that the world will not devote itself to making you happy."

Beyond meaning, mooring and motivation, a sense of mission also gives us *momentum* or speed. Someone once said, "Focus produces velocity." *Having a mission helps you stay focused.*

A mission causes you to set goals that will stretch you beyond what you normally would do, that will get you moving.

In 1519, Cortez landed on the shores of Vera Cruz, Mexico, with seven hundred men ready to seize the country before them. As the men stood facing their new home, smoke from their own flaming ships rose above their heads. Turning around, they saw all eleven ships burning. Cortez shouted,

"Men, don't panic! I set the ships aflame. You see, we only have two options: We take Mexico or we die."

Cortez's men decided they'd better achieve their objective, or they were going to be in deep trouble. Such is the power of a mission.

Do you March to a Mission?

I have adapted some questions from Richard Leider's book *The Power of Purpose* to help you examine this area of mission and purpose in your own life. Answer them by circling *yes* or *no*.

➢ Do you have a clear picture of where you're going? Yes / No

➢ Have you set targets for your life? Yes / No

➢ Are you satisfied with the targets you've set in your personal life? Yes / No

➢ Do you have a written method to track your progress? Yes / No

➢ Are your values clear and sharp in your mind? Yes / No

➢ Have you written down the values you cherish? Yes / No

Where Do I Accomplish My Mission?

So often we only focus on mission in the area of business. Many of my executive friends grow squeamish about developing the same type of mission-mindedness and actual mission plan for their personal lives.

This resistance leads me into my attack mode. I point out how ludicrous it would be to build a business by merely articulating the purpose and vision and then saying, "Okay, troops, go do it." No leader would say that. He or she would move into a very specific strategy in each vital area of concern: production, marketing, finance, administration, sales, etc. Each area would have specific goals along with strategies to accomplish them.

In the same way we all have specific areas in our personal lives that demand attention if we are going to authentically succeed. But we have to identify those areas and develop goals and specific strategies for each one. Take some time to write down all the various roles you play in your life, especially regarding responsibilities.

Just as in your business, you have a role in your family that is specific and vital. Maybe you're the sole provider or sole parent. Maybe you're the encouraging one or the disciplinarian. You have a role as a spiritual leader as well.

If you are going to be effective in accomplishing your mission make certain that you are living a healthy, balanced life.

Your priorities need to be well defined. You need to be focusing on your own growth as well as that of others so that your influence is effective and impactful.

Here are seven key priority areas on which you need to focus:

> **F**aith (spiritual life)
>
> **F**itness (physical and mental)
>
> **F**amily
>
> **F**riendships
>
> **F**inances
>
> **F**irm (career)
>
> **F**un

➤ *Faith.* Begin with your role in relationship to your inner life and contribution (or giving back), because faith entails all of this and it is critical. How do you develop your faith relationship?

➤ *Fitness.* How fit are you mentally, emotionally, spiritually, physically, and professionally? Your overall fitness is important because fitness plays a vital roll in your health and vigor that is essential to your life.

➤ *Family.* Your family will always be a top priority. You may have roles as a spouse, a parent, and also as a child and a sister or brother, with a need to relate to your extended family.

➤ *Friendship.* Friendship includes intimate relationships, casual relationships, neighborhood relationships, and professional relationships.

➤ *Finance.* This area addresses your family or personal budget, taxes, estate, and college-fund planning. It ensures that you keep focused on your short and long-term financial needs.

➤ *Firm* (or career). This category includes all the aspects of your job. You might play many roles as leader, subordinate, peer, teacher, mentor, etc.

➤ *Fun.* This includes hobbies and enjoyable activities where you can really relax and renew yourself.

When and How Do I Accomplish My Mission?

For each role you need to develop specific, logical goals.

➤ What, at the end of your life, will you want to have accomplished in that area?

➤ Which values, character traits, areas of service and spiritual lessons do you want to teach your children?

➤ What legacy do you want to leave?

Once you've written down these specific goals, develop further specific, short-range goals that encompass this year. If one of your goals for your children is for them to become authentic lovers of people—to have a heart and a compassion for others— then what one thing can you do this year to help them develop such compassion? Now move the goal from this year to this week. How can you build something into your schedule *this week* that will begin to achieve this life goal in your children?

Learning to March to a Mission

Once you articulate your mission, how do you learn to "march" to it? There are four basic skills to help you hone your craftsmanship in this area. These skills are: seeing your purpose clearly, wanting it desperately, accomplishing it wholeheartedly, and following it faithfully.

1. See Your Purpose Clearly

You need to know where you're going. You can't win a race unless you know where the finish line is. If you're going to see your purpose clearly, you need to observe several principles.

First, your purpose needs to be very *particular*. You need to specialize your mission statement through goal development. Write out your goals and make them measurable.

✓ Make them specific.

✓ Make them achievable.

✓ Make them inspiring.

Build your goals into your schedule. Being proactive and taking control of your life means you need to have a particular sense of purpose. Grab your destiny! When you wake up in the morning, say, "I am here for this reason," and reiterate your purpose and statement of vision.

Second, you must have a *personal* sense of purpose. Have you ever asked yourself *why* you do what you do?

➢ Why do you spend your money the way you do?

➢ Why do you use your free time as you do?

➢ What causes you to dress as you do?

I am reminded of the man who came home with a roast for his wife to cook for dinner. He watched her slice off the end before she put it in the pot. "Why did you cut off the end of the roast?" he asked her. "I don't know," she said. I've always done it that way."

"But why?" he asked. And, again she said, "I don't know. I just always have. It's the way my mother did it."

So, out of curiosity, he called her mother and asked her why she cut the end off the roast.

She said, "I don't know. Grandma did it, so I do it."

He then called Grandma and asked her why she always cut off the end of the roast and she said simply, "My roaster was always too small."

We often live like that. Why do you spend your money the way you do? Why do you use your free time as you do? Often the reason has nothing to do with your mission in life. Instead, we often do things in a certain way because of what our parents or friends or associates expect of us, or have modeled for us.

A third point is to make your purpose *pre-eminent*. Your mission needs to be the unifying factor around which you organize the rest of your life—and you've got to be willing to pay the price for it. Martin Luther King Jr. said,

"If a man hasn't discovered something he will die for, he isn't fit to live."

2. Want Your Purpose Desperately

This second principle has to do with your *constant* motivation.

➢ How deeply do you desire your mission?

➢ How desperately do you want something?

After you have put your vision, purpose, roles, goals, and guiding principles into print, think about them all the time. Read them over and over. Rehearse them in your mind. Pray for their accomplishment. Talk about them. Interact with people concerning your vision. Tell them what you want to do. Let others hold you accountable.

Remember that life is short. So, accomplish what you truly want to accomplish. Develop a deep sense of the preciousness and shortness of your life. And live in light of that!

3. Accomplish Your Purpose Wholeheartedly

It's a fact that there is a difference between involvement and commitment. W. H. Murray wrote: "Until one is committed there is hesitancy...the chance to draw back...The moment one definitely commits one's self, then providence moves too. All sorts of things occur to help one that would never otherwise have occurred. A whole stream of events issues from the decision raising in one's favor all manner of unforeseen incidents and meetings and material assistance which no man could have dreamt would have come his way."

Learn a deep respect for one of Goethe's couplets:

"Whatever you can do, or dream you can do, begin it. Boldness has genius, power and magic in it."

You must first commit. If you're going to accomplish your purpose wholeheartedly, enthusiastically, and fully, you've got to commit yourself to act.

4. Follow Your Purpose Faithfully

In short, don't quit. Stick with your purpose regardless of whether things are up or down. Booker T. Washington said, "You measure the size of an accomplishment by the obstacles you have to overcome to reach your goals."

There's an interesting caterpillar that lives in the South of Wales. Apparently this caterpillar has no mouth. No digestive system. It is born, reproduces and dies. That's it. Doesn't even eat. Birth...reproduction...and death.

You're placed on this earth for a lot more than that. What's your mission? Take charge right now and complete what you started earlier in this chapter. You will be eternally grateful that you didn't procrastinate on this one!

Why Do You Exist?

How are you doing right now in your application of this principle? Once your commitment to marching to a mission is established, you will have solidified your belief roots. Then you will be free to begin to follow through with right commitments.

Once you've set goals, crafted a mission and started moving quickly towards achieving your dreams you won't want to turn back. Success lies ahead of you, not behind. It waits for you on the horizon.

Go get it!

Action Steps

1. Do you believe you have a purpose in life?

2. What are your unique gifts, abilities, and skills that indicate this sense of purpose?

3. What activities give you the greatest sense of satisfaction?

4. Can you see how they might fit into your mission?

5. What is your innermost desire? What would really make you happy to achieve?

6. Are you working toward that desire which you described in the last question?

7. What do you consider the major roles in your life?

Take the following list of seven areas, and articulate specific activities or interests under each area that you must achieve to fit into the vision of your innermost desire: Faith...Fitness...Family... Friendship...Finances...Firm (Career)...Fun...

"Putting others first is a sign of character...
not compromise!"

Mary Jenson

Section 3

Root Commitments

This final section addresses the basic root commitments you must make and fulfill daily if you are to authentically succeed, if you are to maintain a dynamic, maximized life.

These five principles begin with *Integrate All of Life.* This principle shows you how to sustain dynamic equilibrium in all areas of your life, including your family and career. Moreover, it gives you techniques for balancing your attitudes of structure and spontaneity as well as your goals of results and relationships.

The second commitment principle is *Zero In on Caring for People.* The point of this principle is to learn to love people and use things, not vice versa. This relational principle is often violated, yet you cannot continue to violate it and expect to authentically succeed. This chapter urges you to develop dynamic relationships using skills that create a sprit of unity.

Energize Internally is the third commitment principle. This is your taproot, without which you have no ultimate power. The fact is that without help no one is capable of doing everything we propose in this book. You are a whole person–mind, emotion, body, and soul. All of these human components need to fit and work together for your life to work as a whole. This principle explains how you become character-based and not just performance-led.

The fourth commitment principle, *Realign Rigorously,* details with how to get from point A to point B in the best way possible. Here we explain that life is not a straight path, but a circuitous one. That is, life needs adjustments every day. If you are to authentically succeed at work and at home, you must forever adjust.

The final principle of commitment is *Stay the Course.* The tendency we have when learning any new truth is to try it for a while and then quit from discouragement, boredom, frustration, or simply lack of will. In this chapter we provide very specific craftsman's tools that will enable you to stick with it and become energized.

"Life is like juggling crystal balls and rubber balls; success depends on knowing which is which."

Roy Roberts, Vice President
General Motors Corporation

6

Integrate All of Life

Balancing Life's Demands

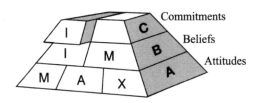

> "If I had my life to live over again, I would dare to make more mistakes next time. I would relax. I would be sillier. I would take fewer things seriously...I would eat more ice cream and less beans. I would perhaps have more actual troubles but fewer imaginary ones. You see I'm one of those people who lived seriously and sanely hour after hour, day after day. I've been one of those persons who never went anyplace without a thermometer, a hot water bottle, a raincoat, and a parachute. If I had to do it over again, I'd travel lighter."
>
> 85-year-old woman from the hill country of Kentucky

Think about the reflection in the words above. Isn't it true we fear that at the end of life we may wish for an altered past? What would you say if you had to finish this sentence?

"If I had my life to live over, I would…"

Now is the time to ask that question so you can begin to live in a deliberately balanced way and avoid any "I wish I would have…" thinking. How would you like your life to be played out? What kind of impact would you like to have? What areas are important to you? How can you integrate all the areas of your life into one great, productive whole?

Harold Kushner wrote: "What is life about? It is not about writing great books, amassing great wealth, achieving great power. It is about loving and being loved. It is about enjoying your food and sitting in the sun rather than rushing through lunch and hurrying back to the office. It is about savoring the beauty of the moments that don't last, the sunsets, the leaves turning color, the rare moments of true communication. It is about savoring them rather than missing out on them because we are so busy and they will not hold still until we get around to them."

What keeps most people from living life to the fullest is usually a preoccupation with one or two aspects of daily life. That's why I want you to look at success in a broader number of areas, not in just one or two. *You cannot call yourself successful when your business is growing but your family is failing.* Success must be balanced. It must be put in the proper perspective.

At one time, people who succeeded in all vital areas of their lives were considered mature and well balanced. These days the rule of thumb is to elevate a successful career (or some other outward goal) above family and personal integrity. Tragically, the idea of balance is reserved for the more public part of our lives:

Do I look fit?

Do I look successful?

Do I look intelligent?

Only to the extent that we manage our personal lives and our family's can we successfully manage in the public arena. To separate the personal and professional is not only dangerous, it's deadly for both individuals and society.

Cross Training

Any person who has been around during the last decades of the twentieth-century or beginning of the 21st century has been bombarded with information about physical fitness and nutrition. Today personal fitness is a multi-billion dollar industry. Everybody seems to have the magic diet, perfect exercise regimen or secret to keeping off those extra pounds. If you've struggled in this area, you've probably tried just about everything, like I have.

Studies show that those who vary their workout schedule with a variety of activities like walking, swimming, weight lifting, rollerblading and cardio dance classes stay committed longer, and are more apt to integrate daily exercise into their schedule. The same can be said for many areas of our lives.

The more we learn to balance our work (firm), family, fitness, fun, faith, finances and friends, the more likely we are to stay motivated, find joy in others and pursue our goals. How many times have you worked like a dog for several days straight so that when you finally got to the weekend you didn't want to move a muscle? We all overdo it sometimes and find ourselves taking a much-needed break, but if this describes your life on a daily basis you need to stop and regroup before you explode.

Cross training in the seven main areas of responsibility can mean the difference between achieving your goals and dropping out of the race. If your priorities, attitudes and goals are in order you'll naturally become a champion cross-trainer, reaching levels of success you never thought possible.

Results of Imbalance

A life lived out of balance is harmful not only to yourself, but also to others. A good example of this is the story of John, an eight-year-old boy, whose parents both work. John's mother is a management consultant who travels frequently.

One night when she arrived home John hugged her and asked why she had been away so long. She replied, "One of the reasons I was away was to make enough money to buy you the bicycle you wanted." John answered back, "Yeah, I really wanted that bike, but moms are more important than bikes. Please stay home more."

Others know when your life is out of balance. Your spouse knows, co-workers know, and if you're honest with yourself, you also know when enough is enough.

All of us are given the same amount of time during each week to get things done: 168 hours. No more. No less. More time is not available. What is available is your opportunity to learn to manage three major areas of your life—priorities, goals and attitudes.

Balancing Priorities—Personal and Professional

Balancing Priorities

The most common area discussed in regard to balance is priorities. Most of us know it is a difficult chore to balance work with the other areas in our lives. If you're going to balance business and other basic relationships, you need to take some definite steps:

1. Rule Your Impulses

The starting point for balancing your priorities is to take charge of your internal drives. You can rule your impulses only by being disciplined.

Be cautious of any type of impulse, including driving yourself. Be careful not to do your work for the purpose of receiving the approval of others or to fill some unmet need in your life. Work was not given to us to meet all of our needs; it simply can't.

Gordon MacDonald, author, pastor, and speaker, uses these qualifications to identify a driven person:

✓ A driven person is most often gratified only by accomplishments.

✓ A driven person is preoccupied with the various symbols of personal accomplishment.

✓ A driven person is usually caught in the uncontrolled pursuit of expansion.

✓ A driven person tends to have a limited regard for integrity.

✓ A driven person often possesses limited or undeveloped people skills.

2. Reorder Your Priorities

The second skill needed in balancing priorities is to place your priorities in the proper order. In *When All You've Ever Wanted Isn't Enough,* Rabbi Harold Kushner reminds us of our need to keep first things first:

> Ask the average man, what is more important to him, making money or being devoted to his family? Virtually everyone will answer family without hesitation. But watch how the average person actually lives out his life. See where he really invests his time and energy, and he will give away the fact that he does not really live by what he says he believes. He has let himself be persuaded that if he leaves for work earlier in the morning and comes home more tired at night, he is proving how devoted he is to his family by expending himself to provide them with all the things they have seen advertised.

> Ask the average woman, what means more to her, the approval of strangers or the affection of people closest to her, and she won't be able to understand why you would even ask such a question. Obviously nothing means more to her than her family and her closest friends. Yet how many of us have embarrassed our children or squelched their spontaneity, when we fear what neighbors or strangers might think? How often have we poured out our anger on those closest to us because we had a hard day at work or someone else did something to upset us? And how many of us have let ourselves become irritable with our families because we were dieting to make ourselves look more attractive to people who do not know us well enough to see beyond appearances?[i]

Underlying Kushner's questions is confusion about priorities. We can vehemently hold to the bottom-line priority, but if we don't live it, we're deceiving ourselves. Think of balance or integration as three concentric circles. The inner circle is your *center* (your core)—that thing, value, spiritual relationship that is the most central part (the boss, or even god, if you will) of your life. The second circle is *you*. The third circle is *others*.

Every day you should nurture and feed each of these three entities. This will liberate you greatly. Cultivate, care for and love your inner center (your god). But, be careful to evaluate what is at your center for this will determine the quality and impact of your life.

Second, you should love yourself. That's right. Love yourself. This does not mean selfish, narcissistic love, the kind that focuses only on your own concerns and interests. It means taking care of yourself. You must develop yourself mentally, emotionally, physically, and spiritually so that you are healthy and can function at an optimal level. Many people spend so much time caring for others or for their work that they let their own lives atrophy. This leads only to devastation in their impact on others. We must be internally healthy in order to win.

Finally, care for, build up, and love others. Where do we find others? They are the people around us—at work, at home, in the neighborhood, at the hardware store, on the tennis court, in our places of worship, even on the freeway.

Every day and all day long we're to nurture our inner core, take care of our minds and bodies, and love and care for others. How? *We do it by recognizing it's not either/or.* People who are after authentic success must work on their spiritual lives, their physical and emotional lives, and the lives of those around them at the same time, all the while accepting that it takes daily, even sometimes hourly, attention.

3. Readjust Your Schedule

Your schedule should revolve around the mission you identified in the last chapter. It should also accentuate the different roles you play. Finally, you should *control your schedule*, not let your schedule control you.

Your schedule should reflect your interests, responsibilities and desires. It should signal that you are giving meaningful time and energy to the seven main areas of life. Again, you are cross training. You are avoiding burn out and you are making the most of your life, pursuing authentic success that is lasting and healthy.

So how do you begin to place your priorities in order?

Take a look again at the list of seven main dimensions in life. Now, without there being a right or wrong answer, rate these seven areas according to which one is most important to you and which one is least. Now ask yourself why you put them in the order you listed.

Faith (spiritual life)

Fitness (physical and mental)

Family

Friendships

Finances

Firm (career)

Fun

Tension is a normal part of life. On any given day, at any given time there are a multitude of decisions to be made.

➢ Whose call needs to be returned before the end of the day?

➢ Which emails should be answered right away?

➢ What should we have for dinner?

➢ How long can Johnny go before he really needs new sneakers?

➢ What should I get my significant other for his birthday?

➢ What's my next step in planning for retirement?

The list is endless, but you don't have to get overwhelmed. If you are practiced in living a balanced life you will know how to prioritize the demands placed on you and you will take pride in your knowledge of how to deal with the most important issues as they rise.

<u>Here are two questions that can help you as you prioritize:</u>

1. What is the greatest need in my life right now?

2. Where has there been previous neglect? What have I let go?

Balancing Attitudes—Structure and Spontaneity

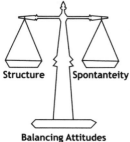

Structure | Spontanteity

Balancing Attitudes

Structure and spontaneity are the tensions that affect our attitudes. Many people lead highly structured lives. They live as if successful time management means getting as much done as possible in every minute of their day. Their written goals lock them into a structure that won't let them go. Structure is important and necessary, but when it becomes the *end* and not the *means* it keeps us from the spontaneity that allows us to buy up the opportunities of life.

Your goal should be to develop some degree of balance between structure and spontaneity. For instance, if you're so busy getting the job done that you can't help your child at a point of his or her need, you'll miss not only the need but also the child. Any time the structure of your work (or life) prevents you from spontaneously loving or caring about another person, you're out of balance. *People are more important than schedules.*

Let me offer you some ways to balance your attitudes. I suggest these three specific steps:

✓ Tighten goals and loosen plans

✓ Think process, not just product

✓ Treat interruptions as guests (respond, don't react)

1. Tighten Goals and Loosen Plans

We mentioned goals earlier. They are like beacons in our lives. They show us a direction. The reticular activator is the portion of the brain that is able to respond to the power of goals.

When you set a specific goal, your mind begins to work toward achieving that goal. One of the great motivating factors in the lives of athletes and other high-performance achievers is that they are able to see very clearly the successful accomplishment of their goal in their mind's eye before they even begin to practice.

2. Think Process, Not Just Product

A second way of balancing your attitudes is by thinking *process* rather than *product*. I believe success is a journey, a progressive realization and internalization of all I was meant to be and do. That means I'm progressively growing intellectually, and I'm progressively growing in my character and conduct.

Indeed, success is tied up in the little moments of the day. It's the little thoughts, the habits, and also our little actions that determine our success. Success is not just the end result, but the process of achieving it as well.

An authentically successful person is one who has found a healthy balance between reaching his or her goals and allowing for spontaneity.

3. Treat Interruptions as Guests

Finally, you should learn to treat interruptions as guests, not as intruders. The unexpected can become the exceptional and change you forever if you let it.

When the unexpected becomes the exceptional in your life, success becomes tangible. Great learning takes place in the process of dealing with interruptions and unforeseen challenges. As we discussed earlier, it is the process, not the product that is important. This becomes a main ingredient in achieving real, lasting authentic success.

Balance Goals—Results and Relationships

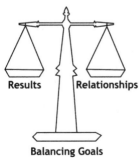

Balancing Goals

We often set goals for work and our professional lives but seldom for our personal and family lives. I've found that my work life will squeeze out my family and personal life UNLESS I schedule dates with my wife, my children, my friends and even myself. I know that if I don't get up in the morning and schedule time to exercise, I won't do it. Also, if I don't work at cultivating my relationship with my wife with a goal of greater intimacy, I won't accomplish that.

So, look at your schedule and set both relational and result goals. I work on setting goals and activities weekly in those 7 key areas—faith, fitness, family, friends, finances, firm (professional life) and fun. Why don't you give it a shot!

1. List Your Goals

Begin by listing your goals, both relational and result-oriented, into your schedule. Most time management is geared toward working on result goals. But let me suggest to you a rather radical paradigm shift: *Implement your goal-setting strategy with your various relationships.* Here are several examples:

- You see an employee or associate who is having difficulty getting along with other people. Therefore, you set a goal and schedule it, aiming to help this person develop relational skills through your mentoring and help.

- You begin to realize that one of your children is developing emotional distance from you. Therefore, you schedule a time to get together with that child and spend concentrated listening and caring time with him or her.

- A good friend has been struggling in a job search. You set a goal and schedule time to call that person and encourage him or her with networking or other help.

- You realize it's been a while since you've taken a deliberate vacation from work (even if only a weekend) or spent concentrated time with certain relatives or friends. So you begin the challenge of scheduling a vacation together with them and you follow through with it!

Who are your friends? Sometimes friendships develop and last with very little attention. But in a mobile society like ours, friendships break up more often than they are supported.

Make a list of those families you hope to have as friends forever. Then drop them a line or call and tell them so. Take charge of this area of your life and watch the results.

2. Listen to Your Intuitive and Logical Mind

A second tool for developing balance in your goals is to listen to both sides of your mind—that is, both the intuitive and the logical. Though the left brain/right brain theory is still being debated, let's assume that the left-brain is logical and likes to accomplish quantitative, measurable goals.

The right brain, on the other hand, is much more intuitive and idea-oriented. It deals with insights and is much more responsive to relational goals. It takes work to adjust throughout the day, to make sure that you don't just restrict yourself to your results-oriented, goal-centered, accomplishment-focused left brain, but that you also allow yourself to reflect, be more intuitive, and more relational.

I regularly see this difference between left and right brain functioning fleshed out in my marriage. I am much more left brain oriented than my wife, Mary. She's the creator, the artist, the one who likes to create atmosphere. She helps me with the intuitive side of life; I help her with left brain tasks. Regardless of our particular giftedness, we all need to learn to listen to both sides of our brains.

3. Love People, Use Things

The final area in which to learn to balance your goals is to learn to love people and use things, not the opposite. Results-driven people often go after things. They love their cars, their boats, their clothes, houses and vacations. They don't always love people, though. Loving people is hard work. It takes concentrated effort and it requires sacrifice and compromise.

The people in our lives cause the most trouble, don't they? If you're not married, you don't have to share the garage. If you don't have children, you won't have to deal with adolescent rebellion. If you don't work with a team, you won't have to share the glory.

But good lives, *right* lives, are not like that. They're made good by the people in them. You will only experience authentic living as you move your attention away from things (and control) as a source of satisfaction and focus on people. Possessions come and go. The only 'things' that count are people.

When we die, we leave it all behind. And before people die, most of them look back and reflect on the same things: family, friends, relationships, impact, quality and character. Those are the real rewards of life, the things that really count. ***How much is your life counting?***

Action Steps

1. Answer the question that you dealt with at the very beginning of this chapter: If I had my life to live over again what would I do differently?

2. Evaluate how well you are accomplishing the three major areas of balance on a scale of 1-5 (1 being poor and 5 being outstanding):

Balancing Priorities (business and basic relationships)

➢ Rule Your Impulses	1	3	5
➢ Reorder Your Priorities	1	3	5
➢ Readjust Your Schedule	1	3	5

Balance Your Attitudes

➢ Tighten Goals and Loosen Plans	1	3	5
➢ Think Process, Not Product	1	3	5
➢ Treat Interruptions as Guests	1	3	5

Balance Your Goals

➢ List Your Goals into your Schedule	1	3	5
➢ Listen to Your Intuitive/Logical Sides	1	3	5
➢ Love People and Use Things	1	3	5

---

[i] Harold Kushner, *When All You've Ever Wanted Isn't Enough* (New York: Simon and Schuster, 1986).

7

Zero In On Caring for People

How to Change People's Lives

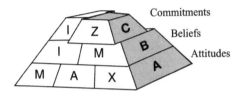

"In the right key one can say anything. In the wrong key, nothing; the only delicate part is the establishment of the key."

George Bernard Shaw

Deep relationships today are not as abundant as they once were. Daniel Yankalovich, in his book *New Rules in American Life*, wrote, "The hunger for deeper personal relationships shows up in our research findings as a growing conviction that a me-first, satisfy-all-my-desires attitude leads to relationships that are superficial, transitory, and ultimately unsatisfying.

"Our surveys show that 75 percent of Americans now recognize that while they have many acquaintances they have few close friends, and they experience that as a serious void in their lives. Moreover, two out of five—41 percent—state they have fewer close friends than they had in the recent past."

You may be like many others in our culture who have lost sight of this fundamental principle of life—the need for caring, building up people, and creating unified teams of productive, affirmed, maximized individuals.

Harold Kushner, the rabbi with such a profound outlook on life, shares a lesson he learned one day at the beach. He was watching two children, a boy and a girl, build an elaborate sandcastle with everything a good castle needs—moats and turrets and passages. Just when it looked as if the castle might be finished, a big wave came unexpectedly and knocked it down. Kushner says he fully expected tears from the children. He was surprised when they laughed, grabbed hands, and moved off to more stable ground to build another castle. Here is the lesson he learned:

"All the things in our lives, all the complicated structures we spend so much time and energy creating, are built on sand. Only our relationships to other people endure. Sooner or later, the wave will come along and knock down what we have worked so hard to build up. When that happens, only the person who has somebody's hand to hold will be able to laugh."

Teamwork

The *Z* in the MAXIMIZERS model, *"Zero in on Caring for People,"* is the key to developing intimate relationships and to changing people's lives. How we change others will be in direct proportion to the level of love we put into our relationship with them. Unabashed caring is the essence of "teamness," which is fundamental for powerful families, friendships, communities, and entire cultures.

Again, Daniel Goleman emphasizes the critical need for interpersonal skills in the development of productive and profitable companies in his landmark published book, *Primal Leadership*. He demonstrates hard evidence that this element of Emotional Quotient (E.Q.) is even more critical than Intellectual Quotient (I.Q.) and often even professional skills, in developing thriving companies.

Jon Katzenbach and Douglas Smith, in their highly popular and influential book, *The Wisdom of Teams*, document powerfully the benefit and absolute necessity of teamness in the business arena. In this fascinating book, the authors list the qualities of powerful teams. One of those qualities is a *"unique social dimension* that enhances the economic and administrative aspects of work.

"Real teams do not develop until the people in them work hard to overcome barriers that stand in the way of collective performance. By surmounting such obstacles together, people on teams build trust and confidence in each other's capabilities. They also reinforce each other's intentions to pursue their team purpose above and beyond individual agendas. Overcoming barriers to performance is how groups become teams. Both the meaning of work and the effort brought to bear upon it deepen, until team performance eventually becomes its own reward."

At their best, these teams are relationally intensive—the members authentically care for one another and build a healthy unity that surpasses normal or even good human relationships.

One of the finest businesses in America is Stew Leonard's supermarket in Norwalk, Connecticut. When asked about the secret to its success, the management said it was people—caring about and serving people.

Whether serving ice cream and cake to those in the checkout line so they wouldn't mind waiting or displaying photos of sixty thousand people who have shopped Stew Leonard's on the back wall, the company demonstrates that it cares. Mr. Leonard himself strolls up and down the aisles asking everyone how he could make grocery shopping more pleasant. His enthusiasm for serving others carries over to his employees who also want to be a part of the good they see.

The rather recent phenomena of networking in the marketplace highlighted for men and women their need to brush up on relational skills. After all, networking is a success or failure based on your ability to work with people. And sooner or later your networking associates often become your friends.

The Ultimate of Teamness: Unity

The real key to this whole concept of teamness lies in the theory of UNITY. Let's put this idea into another acrostic and see if we can begin to work on each element of it to help us achieve our relational goals.

Uplift one another

Need one another

Intimately relate to one another

Trust one another

Yield to one another

Uplift One Another

The place to begin developing unity in relationships is to learn to build up other people. There are two Greek words, *para* and *kaleo*, from which I draw much of this concept's meaning. *Para* means "alongside," and *kaleo* means "to call."

Together these words simply mean putting your arm around someone, calling him alongside, and encouraging him. It means helping to change another's attitude so he or she is willing to go back into battle. It means encouraging, exhorting, and stimulating a person to positive action.

1. Complimenting

The foundational skill needed to uplift those around you is *complimenting*. Mark Twain said,

"I can live for two months on a good compliment."

And Charles Schwab, the great steel executive, noted,

"I have never seen a man who could do real work except under the stimulus of encouragement and the approval of the people for whom he is working."

Learn to compliment people by praising them for something that illustrates their personal and character growth. True compliments encourage people to progress in truth. At the same time, you must consciously determine to express your compliments positively. It's too easy to be sarcastic or flippant.

The American Institute of Family Relations asked parents how many positive and negative statements they made on average to their children. What were the results? The average parent makes ten negative statements to every positive one to his or her children. In another setting, elementary teachers were asked how many positive statements it takes to overcome a negative statement to a child. Research found that it takes four positive statements to overcome every negative one.

Ten negatives to one positive. Four positives to overcome one negative.

Think of those ratios. We can't ignore the impact of our words! You may have grown up in a home where you were put down all your life. As a result, you may have learned the habit of putting down others. Stop doing it. Start uplifting instead.

We train people in this *"Technology of Appreciation"* in our coaching programs. We will ask a team of leaders to go around the room and articulate one thing that they appreciate about one particular person. The other leaders in the room take notes and are often stunned that people say what they say about someone.

They have in many cases just never heard it before. It is not uncommon to have rough, hard men and women become deeply emotional as they hear words of encouragement and appreciation from their colleagues. Give it a shot in your work team and see what happens.

2. Expressing Confidence

A way you can learn to uplift others is to *express confidence* in them. How do you respond when people fail you or your organization? Do you give up on them or shame them? Or do you still try to express some degree of confidence?

Harry Hopman built an Australian dynasty in world tennis. Do you know how he did this? He took a slow player and nicknamed him "Rocket." And he took a weak, frail kid and nicknamed him "Muscles." Rod "Rocket" Laver and Ken "Muscles" Rosewall became two of the greatest tennis players of all time. Why? Someone believed in them.

You can also express confidence in others and articulate appreciation for them through *rewards*. The simple fact is that people do what they will be rewarded for. And one area most of us need to reward more often is risk taking. Too often we discourage risk taking and thereby discourage greatness. Great results often have equally great risks attached to their achievement.

Dale Carnegie said it well:

"Take a chance! All of life is a chance. The man who goes furthest is generally the one who is willing to do and dare. The 'sure thing' boat never gets far from shore."

3. Comforting

The third skill that needs to be sharpened as you learn to encourage people is *comforting.* As difficult as it may be, there are times in our lives when we need to be available to others who are hurting. Sometimes all we need to do is be there and be quiet. Remember, your own tough times can prepare you to empathize with others. So lean into your experiences of grief for the benefit of others.

My good friend John Couch, former General Manager of Apple Computer, tells of his early days at Apple. He extracted great commitment from his people but he was also there for them. Once, one of his key guys went through the loss of his wife. This individual commuted 1-½hours to work and it simply gave him far to much time to think about his loss. Plus going home just depressed him more.

So, John rented an apartment close to work, had the team bring him food and be available 24/7. They didn't say a lot. They didn't need to and he didn't need to hear a lot. But, he needed comfort and he got it.

This is often more difficult for men because we want to "fix" things, especially for our wives. But, we need to learn to just listen at times and care for those people around us. So, fight your tendency to "fix" and turn your pain into gain for someone else by comforting him or her.

4. Coaching

The final way to uplift those around you is coaching. People are encouraged when they see growth in themselves. But growth doesn't just happen. It is ignited and fanned by caring people who help us develop a skill, adjust an attitude, build a mental framework, or gain an insight. These people are coaches.

You are a coach, a mentor, an educator, and a leader. The big question is: How effective are you? A great leader knows the needs of those around him or her and seeks to assist them in their development.

For instance, a great dad will coach his kids—not just in Little League, but also in ...

1. Right values

2. Right attitudes

3. Right commitments

A great business leader will coach and mentor his or her associates and employees in skills and attitudes needed to accomplish their agenda.

How do you coach?

➢ First you determine what is needed.

➢ Then you help people get there through the appropriate means.

It's John Greenleaf's "servant leadership" again. Paul of Tarsus, a figure familiar to those who read the Bible, said, "Warn those who are idle, encourage the timid, help the weak, be patient with everyone." His point? People need coaching in different ways depending on their attitudes and how they best learn.

Use the right method at the right time. If someone is deliberately out of line, admonish that person strongly and deliberately. If someone is overwhelmed, encourage or comfort that person. If someone is weak or given to constant, nagging problems, then come alongside and help him or her.

Hershey and Blanchard popularized the concept of "situational leadership." Their findings can be very simply summarized as follow:

If committed and competent:	Delegate (let them go)
If competent but not committed:	Support (get roadblocks out of their way)
If committed, but not competent:	Coach (show them how)
If not committed or competent:	Direct (tell them why and show them how)

If you have an employee, child, or friend who needs help in some area of life, you can use this specific strategy to be of assistance.

Need One Another

The second major principle in the UNITY acrostic is to develop a healthy interdependence through needing one another. There are healthy and unhealthy ways to relate to individuals. William Glasser in his book *Reality Therapy* maintains that at all times in our lives, we must have at least one person who cares for us and whom we care for ourselves. If we do not have this person, we will not be able to fulfill our basic needs. One characteristic is essential in the other person...her or she must be in touch with reality and able to fulfill his or her own needs in the world.

1. Others Need You

If you have a position of leadership—whether as a parent, an employer, or a manager—it's not hard to believe that other people need you. You are where the buck stops; your feedback is essential. You feel needed. You must fully embrace this reality, privilege, and responsibility if you are going to authentically succeed.

> ➤ *Your family needs you...*
> ➤ *Your friends need you...*
> ➤ *Your coworkers and associates need you...*
> ➤ *Your customers need you...*
> ➤ *Your community needs you...*

Each of these relationships will suffer if you don't accept your place as both a needed and needy human being.

2. You Need Others

We each struggle to recognize our need for other people to keep us in balance, to point out our blind spots, to round out our rough edges and to complement our life. I have learned that seclusion is not the answer and that developing specific friendships has its value. I believe friendships come in three different forms: casual, committed and covenant friends.

The *casual* group represents your acquaintances and the people you see periodically or relate to at a somewhat superficial level. The *committed* friend is one who cultivates your friendship and is there for you. You have significant things in common and like being together. The *covenant* relationship represents those few people in your life (starting with your spouse) who will always be there. These people love you enough to confront you on your soft spots, but still believe in you. They are fans of yours, a support, an encouragement, and a source of open and honest communication. You can struggle together with them.

How do I cultivate each of these friendships? Practice the UNITY acrostic presented above. These principles of caring and establishing unity are what make for vital, deep relationships. And the specific step that has helped me most in developing covenant friendships was my formation of an accountability group. It's easy for me to get off target in the area of needing others, so I have people hold me accountable.

Intimately Relate to Others

Today's culture is not very conducive to intimacy. We're busy people with busy lives. We've got meetings, appointments, commitments and schedules that can't be broken. We may think that we don't have time to get involved with others. We don't have the energy for long-term commitments and we don't have the patience to wait for people who aren't with the program.

Intimacy is the center word of UNITY and central principle in the concept of *zeroing in on caring* for other people. It is central because without it there is no real unity. Remember, unity is oneness—a deep, abiding intimacy.

The point is that intimacy is rooted in effective communication, which involves both *connecting* with someone and being able to *clarify* your position. When two people are able to really get through to one another there is no telling what they can accomplish. A good connection with someone requires openness, honesty and trust. When these three elements are included in your communication, you are then able to clarify your position with confidence. This clarification is a key ingredient for conflict resolution.

1. Connecting

Focus on...	Rather than...
What is being said...	The way it is being said...
The meaning...	The words...
Clarification of valid points...	Defense of incorrect accusations...
Questions...	Indictments...
Understanding...	Judgment...

To connect with people you need to *first* understand their point of view and *then* to communicate clearly your point of view. Did you get the order? Listen first and share second.

Seek To Understand

Work hard to understand the other person's perspective. This doesn't mean that you always agree with that perspective but you must understand it. To accomplish this you will have to truly listen. If being a good listener is not your strongest quality take this opportunity to work on it.

When you exhibit good listening skills you convey a message that the other person is important and worth listening to. Remember the goal of your listening is to understand where another person is coming from. The old saying is true: "While you're talkin' you ain't learnin' a thing." You really want to empathize with him or her. Sympathy is when someone bumps their head on low cabinet and you say, "Oh, I am so sorry." Empathy is when someone hits his or her head and you say, "OUCH!" You *feel* with that person.

If you can accomplish sincere empathy you will be well on the road to connecting. Once someone senses that you truly understand them and accept (not necessarily agree with) their views, they then are ready for you to communicate your perspective.

Dr. John Townsend stated: "We need to accept everyone. We don't have to agree with them or approve of them. Just accept them."

Seek To Be Understood

The second aspect of connecting is your ability to communicate in a way that people clearly understand what it is you are saying and what it is that you mean. What you mean is communicated through your words, tone and body language.

In fact, the percentage is as follows:

> ➤ *7% words...*
> ➤ *38% tone...*
> ➤ *55% body language.*

When someone exhibits strong, confident body language communicating with him or her is easy. You know that the other person is listening and interested in what you have to say.

Do you exude this type of body language? Next time you are engaged in meaningful conversation, take stock of how you are presenting yourself. Self-awareness is a very significant factor in connection.

You must demonstrate this self-awareness with family and close friends as well as with those you think matter, professionally or socially. By knowing your own bents and tendencies, you free yourself up to consider the other perspective.

Effective communication is a complex activity that involves your whole person. So, work hard to get in touch with yourself in such a way that you align your verbal and non-verbal communications. Otherwise you might find that your actions are absolutely sabotaging your intent.

2. Clarifying

Clarifying is the art of focusing on issues in such a way that conflicting perspectives are resolved in the most positive way viable. Sometimes there will be times when you hit an impasse. You can't make someone else respond. All you can do is communicate and clarify in the right way.

Conflict resolution is a hot topic these days. Companies spend vast amounts of resources teaching their employees how to manage their anger, how to properly respond in difficult situations and how to maintain level heads during times of stress. This is particularly difficult in a day and age when people are so afraid to engage in intimate relationships. Communication breaks down and without the true desire to resolve the conflict people fail to resolve their differences in healthy ways.

You know that intimacy is the prerequisite for thriving families, friendships, businesses and communities. And clarification or conflict resolution is critical to this. The fundamental balance in clarification is to speak the truth in love.

Honesty is integral, but it must be held to without intent to harm. You must deal with the real issues, but you must also learn from experience. Remember, conflict is inevitable. It happens in all relationships and is a natural part of the intimacy process.

Not all conflict is bad. Sometimes it helps to make a relationship stronger. It sharpens your character and aids in your development. Don't run from conflict. Instead, use your skills to communicate, connect and clarify.

I'm asked more often than not to address conflict resolution and actually come into conflicted situations to help resolve these conflicts. We have developed a 12-step program to do this, which seems so simple to me. But, what I have learned is that we all bring our own baggage to conflict and that we need a common language. Once I can get a work group or individual to buy into the common language and turn these 12-steps into habits, then they truly begin to resolve conflicts.

Trust One Another

The hinges on the door to intimate, unified relationships are greased by the level of trust you have in and with those around you. This fourth principle involves "believing the best" about people. It doesn't demand that you abandon your discernment of inappropriate behavior. In fact, as mentioned in the previous principle, you must consistently clarify and address conflicts and problems.

This is a HUGE problem in the corporate world. I'm stunned at how much time we spend coaching our clients on learning just how to listen and empathize. We get outstanding training in our field of professional expertise but it seems that increasingly people have not been trained to listen. Listening is critical to effective communication and is foundational to healthy productive companies.

Trust underscores the need to avoid developing harmful misconceptions about others—misreading nonverbal communication, misjudging motives, or making false accusations. Forming preliminary assumptions is a sure way of closing another's spirit—not only stopping present communication but hardening the arteries of its future flow.

Yield to One Another

Now, this last letter in the UNITY acrostic may not sound too appealing to you. But if you really want to change people's lives, you learn to yield to them. You may say, "That's stupid!" It's not stupid. Continual fighting produces only bruises, breaks, and resistant people. But when you learn to yield appropriately, at the right time, you'll take all the hot air out of an argument and allow others to respond positively.

Real commitment is seen in our willingness to yield. This spirit is evidence of a selfless, caring love for others. Without it, you communicate merely a self-centered, ego-driven, superficial relationship, which is based on outward conditions and performance, not real commitment.

How do you yield to others?

You submit yourself to those absolute principles that govern your thoughts, emotions, and behavior. You do it every day—at work, at home, in social settings, even on the road.

Imagine this scenario at home: You're late—again—and during dinner your wife says,

"When are you going to get your priorities straight and give some attention to me and your children?"

How would you feel?

Angry, embarrassed, bitter?

And what would you normally do? Yell back?

"Look! I'm the one who keeps food on the table." Or, "Why don't you get a job so I don't have to work extra hours?" Or, perhaps more likely, "Shut up!"

From *Character Counts* on KNBC News comes and interesting account of a father and a son. A 10 year-old-boy approached his father at the dinner table and asked the dad, who was a high-powered attorney with a big law firm that consumed many hours of the father's time, how much his father made an hour as a lawyer.

The father decided he would share this information with his son. He was growing up and was entitled to ask such a question. He told him that he charged $200 per hour.

The son then said, "Dad, can you lend me $100?" The father came down hard on the son and simply said,

"No, I won't do such a silly thing. We *earn* money around here!" The boy left the table and went to his room.

The father finished eating, got up and as he passed by his son's bedroom door he heard sobs. He knocked and opened the door. There seated on the bed was his son with tears in his eyes. The father knew it had to do with the asking of a loan, so he said,

"Jimmy, why do you want to borrow $100?" The boy answered through his sobs,

"Dad, I've saved up $100 and all I need is another $100 to buy an hour of your time." The humbled father yielded to the son.

Let me suggest a radical strategy. *Yield.* That's right—yield. I don't mean to imply that your spouse is totally right and that you are totally at fault. But think of the message you convey to your wife or husband and children, if you yield.

Does yielding always produce fruit? Does it always repair a relationship? Certainly not. Yet it is the only way of *potentially* producing that kind of fruit and authentically succeeding at creating *unity.*

> ➤ Do you want to make a difference in people's lives?
> ➤ Are you willing to set aside your own agenda and to encourage the success of others?
> ➤ Do you want to zero in on caring for people? You know what you have to do.

You have to relinquish your own will, your own way, and your own wisdom at times. You've got to give preference to others.

You can make a difference in their lives!

Action Steps

Uplift One Another

➢ Identify the two most critical people in your life—one from your personal life and another from the professional side. Recalling the four sub-principles of Uplifting One Another (complimenting, expressing confidence, comforting, and coaching), what specific step can you take this week to begin to create the "right key"?

➢ Determine where you can practice each of the four sub-principles this week.

Need One Another

➢ Who are the six most critical people who need you at home and at work?

➢ Who are your committed friends?

➢ Who are your covenant friends?

Intimately Relate to One Another

➢ In which specific relationships do you need to become more vulnerable to enjoy closer friendships?

➢ How can you display this openness?

➢ Identify one major conflict that needs clarification.

Trust One Another

➢ Identify one area where you have violated this principle. What will you do to resolve it?

Yield to One Another

➢ Where must you put this principle to work? With a boss, a friend, a coworker, a spouse, a child?

➢ Identify your strategy (time, place, conversation, etc.). Do at least one thing this week to demonstrate yielding. The principle works with anyone you encounter, any place, anytime.

"You measure the size of an accomplishment by the obstacles you have to overcome to reach your goals".

Booker T. Washington

8

Energize Internally

How to...
Experience Ultimate Personal Power

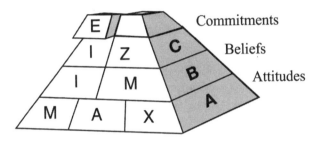

"...in the midst of economic plenty we starve spiritually."

David Myers

L isten to Jeff, a single, twenty-six-year-old advertising executive, who has been successful in many ways and yet feels a spiritual vacuum, even while enjoying the best of times:

My life has been terrific the last few years—lots of money, women, friends, all sorts of activities and travel. My job is good and I am good at it. There is even a good future—I will probably be promoted this year and make lots more money and have freedom to do what I want. But it all seems to lack any significance for me. Where is my life leading? Why am I doing what I'm doing? I have the feeling that I am being carried along without ever making any real decisions or knowing what my goals are. It's sort of like getting on a road and driving along fine, but not knowing why you chose that particular road or where it is leading.

In your concentration on the roots of your life, *energizing your inner life*—dealing with that spiritual vacuum in order to answer your questions of significance—is the taproot. A taproot is the "main root of a plant, usually stouter than the lateral roots and growing straight downward from the stem." Without it, the rest of the plant will quickly rot and die.

All the principles within the MAXIMIZERS model have significant stand-alone value. But this principle of energizing the inner life and its accompanying implications are absolutely necessary to accomplishing the overall goals we've established.

In order to really live out the principles we've been talking about, you must have an irrepressible, inner strength that flows from your character and an ever-deepening spiritual core. Your character is the root of that strength—and your spiritual core is that which brings life to the root. So, if you can focus only on one principle, this is it!

Let's take an example of an historical figure that lived nearly three thousand years ago. His name was Solomon and he reigned as Israel's wisest and most magnificent king. Historical records, including the Bible, record that God appeared to him early in his career and asked him to name anything he wanted. Solomon requested only a discerning heart, that he might rule the nation with justice. As a result, people from around the world came to consult this great king. Because Solomon was blessed with such wisdom, he also became a man of many possessions. He had it all! Consider this list:

He built magnificent cities and structures (the temple and Solomon's palace). He had unparalleled wealth (1400 chariots, 12,000 horsemen), was the author of 3,000 proverbs and 1,005 songs (*Proverbs, Song of Solomon, Ecclesiastes*), was an expert in botany and zoology. He had the dubious distinction, but proof of success in those days, of having 700 wives and 300 concubines.

But, even though Solomon had many possessions, history records that he departed from his spiritual roots—and the net result was increased flaws in the fabric of his character. The ultimate effect was a divided kingdom, a lost empire, family destruction, and personal depression, shame, and grief. Summing up his life and all that it gave him, Solomon wrote these words: "Meaningless! Meaningless! Everything is meaningless...a chasing after the wind."

At the end of the book of *Ecclesiastes*, which describes the ups and downs of Solomon's life, he shares his final words of wisdom: "Now all has been heard; here is the conclusion of the matter: Fear God and keep His commandments, for this is the whole duty of man. For God will bring every deed into judgment, including every hidden thing, whether it is good or evil."

Solomon implied that only two worthy pursuits exist: "Fear God" (cultivate your spirituality) and "keep His commandments" (cultivate character by obeying truth).

Why is This Principle so Critical?

1. It is the Source of Our Strength

The title of this chapter says it in a nutshell: your character energizes your life. Your power and ultimate success will flow out of your character—that is, who you are on the inside—and this character is profoundly influenced by your spiritual depth and maturity.

Stephen Carter in *The Culture of Disbelief* and Bill Bennett in *The Book of Virtues* have powerfully made the case for this source of energy for life. Both of these books have been big sellers; the latter was number one on the *New York Times* Best-Sellers List for more than twenty weeks.

Why? Because people are looking for deeper and more profound answers to the growing problems of our day. Years of abandoning the development of character and spirit have left an empty generation, with little or no strength to face life as we now know it.

What measure of abundance and strength we *do* have today, and all our many, many freedoms, are due to the attention to character of earlier generations. In essence, we are leeching off the lives of our ancestors and leaving our culture in ruin.

Alexander Solzhenitsyn spoke in his 1978 Harvard commencement address of the West's "spiritual exhaustion." The great Russian writer said,

"In the United States the difficulties are not a Minotaur or a dragon—not imprisonment, hard labor, death, government harassment and censorship—but cupidity, boredom, sloppiness, indifference. Not the acts of a mighty, all-pervading, repressive government but the failure of a listless public to make use of the freedom that is its birthright."

2. It is the Basis for Enduring Societies

Consider America's spiritual roots. Our significant decline as a country can be directly related to our increasing abandonment of our spiritual roots. A helpful starting point is to remember where we have come from.

Have you ever wondered why America's population of just three million in the 1770s produced such brilliant leaders as Thomas Jefferson, Benjamin Franklin, George Washington, John Adams, James Monroe, James Madison, and a host of others? Can you come up with a similar list, in our population of over 250 million, that can compete with the list above?

In answering this question, Zig Ziglar, the popular sales trainer, posed the question: "Could it be that what those early Americans were taught had a direct bearing on their performance and accomplishments?

"For example, according to the Thomas Jefferson Research Institute, in the 1770s over 90 percent of our educational thrust was aimed at teaching moral values. At that time most of the education was handled in the home, church, or in church-supported schools. By 1926 the percentage of moral training had been reduced to 6 percent, and by 1951 the percentage was so low you could not even measure it."

Consider the words of George Washington in his first inaugural address. He pledged, "that the foundations of our national policy will be laid in the pure and immutable principles of private morality…."

He further proclaimed,

"There is no truth more thoroughly established than that there exists in the economy and course of nature an indissoluble union between virtue and happiness."

Or reflect on the sentiments of the great Abraham Lincoln: "The only assurance of our nation's safety is to lay our foundation in morality and religion." The point is obvious: Character-centeredness flowing from spiritual roots is the ultimate source of our power individually, institutionally, and socially.

Therefore, I contend that you must weave this principle into the fiber of your life. Your spiritual roots will empower the growth of your character through the establishment of moral bearings, daily internal reformation, heightened perspective, and the control of your basic impulses. They will root you! And unless you accept this premise, you will overlook the very taproot of your life and never experience ultimate power.

3. It's the Secret to Our Satisfaction

Character-centeredness is not only the source of real strength but also the key to a life of satisfaction. In his outstanding book *The Pursuit of Happiness*, David Myers addresses what makes people happy. This becomes clear in the subtitle of his book, "Discovering the pathway to fulfillment, well-being and enduring personal joy."

Dr. Myers takes a scientific-research approach to measuring happiness, and his discoveries align very closely with my research on authentic success. He concludes that happiness and fulfillment are by-products of certain attitudes and perspectives, and not significantly affected by externals. Dr. Myers then elaborates extensively on how and where these traits are developed. He begins with a discussion on the decline in materialistic values, citing Ronald Inglehart's worldwide studies of shifting values:

"We see this most clearly in the demise of secular Marxism in Eastern Europe. But in the West, too, a new generation is maturing with decreasing concern for economic growth and social order...and with increasing concern for political freedom, personal relationships, and the integrity of nature.

This emerging *post materialism* provides fertile soil for a new consciousness that questions prosperity without purpose, money without meaning. After two decades of rising concern for "becoming well-off financially," the percentage of American collegians rating this a very important life goal finally began to taper off during 1989 and 1990.' Concludes Inglehart, 'A renewed concern for spiritual values' is beginning."[i]

Why do researchers find such positive links among spiritual values, mental health, and happiness? Because spiritual values and spirituality provide...

➤ A place to belong (community)

➤ A sense of purpose (commitment)

➤ A perspective on life (contentment)

People with spiritual values are drawn together in community by their sense of common purpose, by a mutual belief in a higher cause. This commitment to the cause *and* the community around them provides the kind of perspective on life that produces a healthy view of self, life and eternal issues. From that perspective and support comes contentment, a conviction that relationships and life itself are worth the work.

Spiritual depth makes the difference in this process. It stimulates and feeds the roots of authentic success. Cultivating the spiritual and character base in your life is both beneficial and *necessary*.

Concentrate on Being

Energizing your inner life involves at least two specific needs: your need to *concentrate on being*, and your need to *cultivate spirituality*.

We are a nation of people consumed with "having." We not only want to have material things, but knowledge and information as well. We even want to have the intangibles of love, inspiration, and happiness. Ownership seems to be the king of virtues, no matter what the commodity, and yet we are a society of notoriously unhappy people—lonely, anxious, depressed, and dependent. In fact, we are learning that the more we have, the less satisfied we are.

If we're going to concentrate on "being," we need to begin with the internals—character. Instead, because we have become so preoccupied today with how we appear in public, we tend to focus on our outward performance not our inner character. This often results in pretending to be someone we aren't. We project one life and live another. This results in a lack of internal motivation and power to live and behave the way we ought. It also results in manipulation of others.

That's why we need to get back to character. We must live from the inside out. There are numerous character qualities that we ought to be developing. Taking clues from the great philosophers, religious statesmen, and successful leaders, we can boil these desirable character qualities down to a focus on the concept of authenticity.

To be authentically successful, you must be the same on the inside as you are on the outside. This means being a person of integrity. You must align your inner, private life and outer, public life around the same principles. It is from here that real energy flows. Some of the most ludicrous logic on this matter has come from Washington, D.C. In defense of their incongruous lifestyles, many of the nation's leaders have tried to convince us that their private lives are not a matter having any bearing on their performance at work.

In the corporate world, despite appearances to the contrary, one study of CEOs from Fortune 500 companies indicated that the most critical factor to consider in hiring or promoting top managers and in gauging their potential for ultimate success is integrity. Ironically, the integrity some CEOs look for in new employees is absent in the topmost ranks. Also, interestingly, traits that were ranked as least important were appearance, likeability, and conformity. I find it interesting that the characteristics many adolescents, the general public, and the mass media find most attractive are the least likely to lead to genuine, enduring success.

A story is told of a young nurse who was completing her first day of responsibility in the operating room of a large, well-known hospital. "You've only removed eleven sponges, doctor," she told the surgeon. "We used twelve."

"I removed them all," the doctor declared. "We'll close the incision now."

"No," the nurse objected. "We used twelve sponges."

"I'll take the responsibility," the surgeon said grimly. "Suture!"

"You can't do that!" blazed the nurse. "Think of the patient."

The surgeon smiled, lifted his foot, and showed the nurse the twelfth sponge. "You'll do," he said.[ii]

Make a commitment to be consistent—inside and outside. The focus of this consistency must be based on your own value system. That should wake you up! Everyone has a value system, whether it is determined thoughtfully or thoughtlessly. And we live out our value system either intently with determination, or haphazardly with no attention at all. It is critical that you choose to center your life around lasting, right, honorable, carefully researched and specifically chosen values.

Now, take the values statements you developed under the principle of internalizing right principles (chapter 4). Ask yourself whether those values are just statements on paper or practices you are consistently building into your life. The first area you must concentrate on is *being*—who you are, your character. Next, let's explore the area of spirituality, because the flame of character needs the fuel of spirituality.

Cultivate Spirituality

You may be a person who has never been religiously oriented. But what I am talking about here is spirituality, not religion. Let me show you the distinction. When I think of spirituality, I think of our internal issues. When I think of religiosity, I think of externals. When I think of spirituality, I think of relationships—our personal and private relationship with a supreme being and our relationships with others in light of that. When I think of religiosity, I think of rules.

Spirituality	Religiosity
Internal character	External performance
Relationship with God and others	Rules
Progressive and growing	Pretense to perfection and fixed
Openness and transparency	Pretentious and closed
Attractive and compelling	Pushy and offensive

When I think of religiosity, I think of people trying to be perfect and never making it. When I think of spirituality, I think of transparency, openness, and honesty.

When I think of religiosity, I think of a facade—people trying to hide things because of their weaknesses. When I think of spirituality, I think of being winsome, attractive, and compelling.

Spirituality is progressing, growing, and developing in that personal relationship between a supreme being and your inner center. By the way, whatever is at your center (your core) is your boss. Another word for boss is god. So, you *do* have a boss or a god of some type. You simply need to decide who or what that god is going to be. It is one of the most importance decisions you'll ever make.

The word spirit, among other things, means also a "vital principle or animating force with living beings." Best-selling author Sam Keen has another definition of spirituality: "In every cycle of breath, between the emptying and the inflowing, there is a moment of absolute calm, an instant when history comes to an end. Then, the yearning begins, the divine discontent, the lungs praying to be filled, the body longing to be animated by spirit."

How can you cultivate spirituality? Let me suggest three simple steps.

1. Reflection

The first step is to learn to experience your own center or higher being if you chose through reflection. Not necessarily formal, organized reflection. Simply open, honest conversation…sharing your needs, desires, wants, joys, sorrows, frustrations, and expectations.

"I seek to enter the morning slowly," says best-selling author and speaker Ken Blanchard, author of *The One Minute Manager*. My friend Ken, like many others I have interviewed and researched over time, spends from fifteen minutes to two hours in daily solitude, reflection, and prayer.

As one leader said, "I have so much to do that I must spend one hour in meditation and prayer if I am going to get it all done." His point is clear. This time of prayer and reflection, gives him the perspective, power and peace, to not only do things right but to do the right things.

One leader of a three-billion-dollar corporation said that he goes through his Day Timer daily, reflecting on the previous day's schedule to determine whether he had perhaps been offensive, inappropriate, rude, or unloving to someone in the course of the day. If he had, he asks forgiveness from God and, if necessary, from the other person. He mentioned that he believes such times give him real clarity to function effectively at home and at work.

Others communicate their habit of spiritual interaction throughout the day—simply offering up words of thankfulness, concerns, struggles and joys. Their consistent assessment is that these times of active dependence on a greater source than yourself are the *keys* for overall effectiveness in their lives and in the lives of any who incorporate spiritual interaction into the warp and woof of living.

So, become a person of spiritual interaction. Begin with some daily time of solitude. Then simply talk to your god throughout the day, just as you would to a friend.

2. Meditate on Great Principles

The second thing we can learn to do is to meditate. There are two basic ways to think about meditation. One philosophy, from Eastern thought, assumes that god is everywhere and if we *empty* our minds, god or the ultimate spiritual being within us will raise us to a higher level of understanding.

The other primary philosophy comes from Hebraic thought. Ancient Jewish writers spoke about meditating on the Law, or principles, day and night. The assumption is that emptying our minds, if that is ever truly possible, leaves us with nothing save our own limited resources.

What a person needs to do instead is to fill his or her mind with right thoughts that will positively influence his or her lifestyle. Meditate on great thoughts and truths that help you grow, develop, and build character into your life.

Read the great books and thinkers—Shakespeare, Melville, Socrates, Plato, Aristotle, the Bible, etc.

Learn to meditate. Make it a habit day and night. Allow yourself time in the morning to focus on planning, and perhaps some time to mull over a few of the deeper truths that have enriched humankind. You may also want to stop in the middle of the day to "smell the roses," acknowledging the wonder of the world around you.

Finally, before you go to bed, reflect on the day, focus on the kinds of thoughts that make life meaningful to you. Watch what happens as you're changed from the inside out.

3. Express Your Faith

You also can cultivate spirituality by expressing faith. Briefly explained…faith is your belief that positive things can come out of wherever you are in life.

However, faith is only as good as the object in which it is placed. I urge you to think long and hard about the source of your faith.

Ask this:

➢ Is this faith historically credible?

➢ Do I see evidence of changed lives because of this faith?

➢ Does this faith adequately address the core issues in my life—meaning, forgiveness, power, direction, and values?

The effectiveness of your faith is in direct proportion to your sense of the reality of a living spiritual being. Faith is like a muscle: The more you use it, the bigger and stronger it grows.

Professionals in many fields acknowledge the need for spiritual growth in human beings. You can build a relationship with God the way you build a relationship with any close personal friend. It can be meaningful. It can be significant. It can be deepening. And it can be yours.

You can talk about it if you want to, or you don't have to talk about it if you don't want to. Just enjoy it and let your spirituality grow and be cultivated.

Regardless of how you define faith, you are a spiritual and physical person. You need to get in touch with what and/or who is at your inner center. For that will be your power source.

Start flexing your faith muscle. Read inspirational writings, meditate on great thoughts, stop to reflect, and seek to go deeper. Watch your life change for the better!

Action Steps

➤ How are you different in your character (the real you) and your personality (external projection) in the following areas?

- o Character (inner self)
- o Personality (outward self)
- o Personal life
- o Family life
- o Business life
- o Social life

➤ How can you create alignment in one of these areas this week? Develop and implement an action plan.

➤ Which of the three spiritual development skills do you need to focus on at this time? What fifteen-minute-a-day practice can you implement to begin a twenty-one-day experiment in making a habit of this skill?

---

[i] Ronald Inglehart in David Myers, *The Pursuit of Happiness* (New York: Avon Books, 1992), pg. 179.

[ii] Jeffrey P. Davidson, "Integrity: The Vanishing Virtue," *PMA Adviser V,* 9:1.

9

Realign Rigorously

Getting from Point A to Point B the Right Way

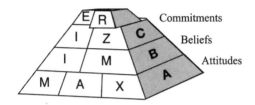

"For a conscious being, to exist is to change, to change is to mature, to mature is to go on creating oneself endlessly."

Henri Bergson

Y ou've probably seen the speedway game that kids play in video arcades. Maybe you've tried it. You press the button, and suddenly the images on the screen start moving toward you. You steer your video car around obstacles, you speed up, you slow down, you adjust to quick changes, and sometimes you crash. And in the next round you raise your skill level: You gain momentum. There are still obstacles that confront you, yet you are more able to handle the changes per unit of time.

What does it take to stay on the track in this game?

A lot of attention and constant mid-course corrections. And so it should be in your work and personal life. That's the principle I am going to discuss in this chapter—how to *realign your actions rigorously*, or, how to get from point A to point B the right way.

Many of us think the old, straight-line approach to getting anywhere is the only right way. But life isn't like that. At times life is messy. So mid-course corrections are necessary to a successful, maximized life.

We've got to learn how to respond to the needs around us and revise our actions rigorously and consistently. We do this by practicing three skills...*framing, focusing and flexing.*

Framing

Framing is developing your overall perspective and sense of parameters about any issue in life. Whenever you face a problem or decision, you need to begin by forming your framework. What's your frame? What are your guides? What will give stability to any decision you make?

Framing entails four major aspects, which become clearer if you can picture the four sides of a picture frame: your overarching *purpose* in this situation and in your life, your *priorities* in this situation and in your life, your *principles* or guidelines in this situation and in your life, and finally, your *peculiarities* (the differences and distinctions that make you up, including your strengths and weaknesses) in the situation and your life.

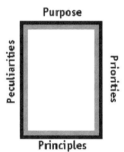

1. Purpose

The first thing you must do to frame your situation is to understand your *purpose* in making this decision as it relates to your overarching sense of purpose and mission in life.

That's where you get back to this whole area of setting your mission statement in the form of specific goals. Where do you want to go? What do you see as the ultimate outcome of your life? Your personal life...your marriage...your business...your friends...your contribution? Develop that sense of vision so you know where you are going.

The founder of IBM, Thomas Watson, was asked once when it was that he began to see the enormous success IBM would become. He said, "Right from the beginning." That's true of great leaders. They get a vision of what they want to accomplish and faith in that vision spurs them on.

For instance, let's imagine that a decision you have to make has to do with correcting somebody in the workforce. You're trying to decide how to do this. The place to start is to ask...

> ➢ What is *my* purpose here?

> ➢ What am *I* trying to do?

Asking questions like that, and making yourself answer them, requires you to be thoughtful and keeps you from merely reacting.

It's the "count to ten" mentality with the extra benefit of growth thrown in. If your overarching purpose is to help individuals grow (because of your commitment to *zero in and care for people*) and thereby encourage growth and development in the organization, how you approach a situation that requires correcting someone will be dramatically affected by your answer.

This concept of purpose allows you to see the forest while you're dealing with one of the trees. And if your perspective isn't big enough, you could miss the opportunity and may make a decision that might have devastating consequences down the road.

2. Priorities

The second major area of framing is the skill of *prioritization*. We've already talked about developing priorities in life under the principle of "integrating all of life." If you've clearly developed your prioritization built on the paradigm I have recommended—you will have a healthy foundation as you move forward to make your decision.

You also need to understand your priorities in a given situation. For instance, if in correcting someone, you elevate the circumstances higher than your regard for the person you are correcting, you run the risk of making a major dent in your relationship and possibly creating devastating consequences.

3. Principles

The third area of framing is to lean into your *principles*. I see principles like train tracks. A train has a hard time moving without those tracks. Sometimes we try, like a train without tracks, to move ahead without having underlying principles to guide us. And though you might view tracks as restricting the freedom of the train, they actually give it freedom to move ahead all the more rapidly. In the same way, principles that are rooted in absolutes will guide you in getting the job done more effectively and will allow your mental agility to really come into play.

If you don't have principles deeply imbedded in your life you will lack direction, wisdom and balance. Just as the train needs tracks that are running parallel, so you need principles to guide you. Often, these are seemingly opposites held in tension. Let me illustrate.

If you want to resolve a conflict, don't do what most of us do—practice flight (run away, hide, deny, repress, suppress the issue) or practice fight (yell, scream, be abusive emotionally, mentally or physically, or be offensive). Both of these are wrong.

Wisdom and *principled living* demands that you speak the truth (this stops the flight). But you must also speak truth with respect (this stops the fighting). Those two principles need to be held in tension in order to experience the freedom of the rails and a smooth flowing life filled with meaningful, rich and productive relationships.

4. Peculiarities

Finally, you frame by understanding your own *peculiarities*. We talked about this somewhat under principle two, "Achieving Personal Significance," when you looked closely at your personal strengths and weaknesses.

In this situation, you'll want to know what your weak tendencies might be in a particular circumstance. For instance, in confronting someone, you may have a basic weakness in speaking the truth because of an underlying desire to be liked. Actually, at the root of this is an integrity problem.

If this is the case, be careful. You may need to have someone else with you at first when you're dealing with confrontation problems. Or, you may need to write down your words ahead of time so that you can, with integrity, be truthful as well as compassionate. Then, you may need a friend or associate to hold your feet to the fire to ask you specifically what you said. You can do all of this to protect yourself and others from your weakness.

To help you better know how to deal with these situations, you should have advisors of your own that you can go to for insight. First, you should have a personal mentor or counselor. This is a friend who knows you well and cares enough for you that he or she can speak the truth to you about your strengths and weaknesses, your consistencies and inconsistencies.

Second is a spiritual counselor. This is a person of sound understanding and wisdom; someone whom you believe understands truth and will serve as a coach or counselor to you. This is a principled person who has integrity and who will help you grapple with the issues.

The third type of consultant or counselor is a specialist in the area of your concern. For instance, if you're focusing on a family problem, you may want to locate a family counselor or specialist. If you're dealing with an area of management and strategic planning, you may want a strategic planning specialist. Look for a pro in whatever field you want to address.

The fourth and final type of consultant you want is a practical counselor. This is someone who is a nuts-and-bolts, practical person—an individual who'll say either, "It will work," or, "It won't work," or, "This doesn't make sense," or, "Great idea, but it's just armchair philosophy."

Focusing

The second major issue I want to address is the importance of *focus*. Focus is the ability to keep your eye on your goal *and* the task at hand, while at the same time being mentally agile in dealing with the various contingencies that come into play. "Laser-like focus is perhaps the most common trademark of the super-successful," writes Robert Ringer in his fine work, *Million Dollar Habits*. He adds that "the more certain you are about your purpose in life, the more focused you'll be on living in the present and the more enthusiastic you'll be in your day-to-day work; the more you display enthusiasm in your daily work, the more likely you will attract the attention of positive, enthusiastic people."

1. Concentration

Karl Vesper of the University of Washington illustrates the importance of attention in making key business innovations. He writes in his book, *New Venture Strategies*:

- Leo Gerstenzang thought of Q-Tips when he saw his wife trying to cleanse their baby's ear with toothpicks and cotton.

- Ole Evinrude got angry when the ice cream in his rowboat melted before he got to his island picnic spot, so he invented the outboard motor.

This next account may grab your attention: A chemist who wanted to teach his ten students the power of observation and focus said to them, "Do exactly as *I* do." He took a specimen bottle filled with (you guessed it) specimen. Then he stuck his forefinger in the bottle, took it out, and stuck his middle finger in his mouth. He told his students to do exactly as he had done. The students freaked out! They thought he had stuck his forefinger in the specimen bottle and then put the same finger in his mouth. So, one by one they all went around and did just that. How disgusting! The professor watched them. Then, after explaining their mistake, he said, "Ladies and gentlemen, you've got to focus."

2. Constant Learning

We read a great deal today about the "constantly learning company." This is a modern movement that flows from the "quality management emphasis" popularized by Dr. W. Edwards Deming in his historic work in Japan. "Learning companies" are organizations skilled at creating, acquiring, transferring knowledge, and modifying behavior to reflect new knowledge and insights. Why this new emphasis on learning? The fact is, our compiled knowledge doubles every year. An advanced degree in any discipline will hold its value for only about six to eight years. In higher technology, knowledge is replaced every two to three years.

Given these rapid refresh rates, knowing *how* to learn is a key to the future. Learning companies measure learning using the half-life curve, or the time it takes to achieve a 50 percent improvement in a specified performance measure such as defects, on-time production, and time-to-market. That is, bottom-line events are tied to the learning curve.

The critical difference in learning companies is that the *spirit* of learning is encouraged. Each learning step is reinforced with multiple methods at every level, and systems are vested to support the changes.[i]

Some organizations defend against change because they are made up of individuals who are working at what "always has worked." Many companies, like many individuals, think that to change means *they have been wrong all these years.* Not so. In the same way that companies must constantly be learning, so must you.

To focus your learning, think through these points:

> ➢ Know what is important to know.

> ➢ Discipline your reading and mental focuses toward those things that will help you accomplish your overarching mission in life. (Certainly, you are free to be entertained mentally; relaxation and refreshment are part of any growth.)

> ➢ What principle does this information support or violate?

> ➢ Is this information a universal truth (an absolute) that is always true in every circumstance?

> ➢ Under what subcategory of the MAXIMIZERS principles does this information fit? (For example, under *Achieving Personal Significance*, does it fit under your specialness or your soft spots?)

Understand what is meant by the information. Read, watch and listen critically. Try using a pen or marker when you read to highlight points. Then interact mentally with what you read. I often debate the author of a book as I read and write down my points of contention in the margins.

Decide what to do with this data. There is little as sad to me as someone who is filled with knowledge and either does not know how to apply it or just won't.

Flexing

Finally, I want to address the importance of *flexing.* You must master the ability in any decision-making situation to constantly adapt to change and to adjust to mistakes in an appropriate way.

Flexibility, or mental agility, is what Charles Garfield defines in his highly popular book, *Peak Performers*, as "the [ability] to change perspective and do the creative thinking necessary to deal with challenges."

Earlier I talked about routinely asking the questions: "What have I neglected in the past?" and "What are the present needs?" This takes mental agility. I'm not suggesting you dodge thoughts or feelings, but rather that you allow yourself to see things in perspective.

Try to describe things as accurately as you can to yourself and to others so that you can get the best possible perspective on them.

1. Creativity

Creativity is not always found in an environment of tranquility and ease. In fact, a creative environment is often a quite chaotic and messy one. Remember: To get the paste out of the tube, you have to squeeze a little.

Creativity is the ability to see things in a new way. It is taking a fresh look at the familiar. Public relations executive John Budd wrote, "Creativity is the result of intense focus on a particular problem. It's a logical thought process that maneuvers towards a solution. It occurs not because a person is trying to be original but because a person is attempting something difficult. A truly creative person excludes conventional solutions and searches beyond them."

Everyone has the potential for creativity. It is possible for everyone to enhance it, nurture it, and let it flourish, or to block and suppress it. If you are conscious of these conditions, you will either fear or facilitate its emergence. How creative are you?

2. Adaptability

Another aspect of flexibility is adaptability. This is the ability to handle ambiguities. Years ago there was an article in the *Harvard Business Review* that listed qualities of outstanding CEOs. One of the major strengths of these executives was the ability to live with ambiguity for an extended period of time while focusing on the ideal.

Isn't that something? *We want life to be neat; we want to travel in a straight line. But that's not how it works.*

People aren't alike. We're all different, and we all tend to push buttons in each other. Consequently, certain situations and people drive us crazy. Therefore, identifying problem situations and finding a creative way around them will give you a flexibility that's necessary for mid-course corrections. This applies not just to your work situation, but to your home and your personal life as well.

If you can learn to apply these principles in your life, you'll be the kind of person who is truly moving toward authentic success. And you'll be in a position to follow the final principle of this book—to stick with it and *stay the course.*

Action Steps

➤ List any challenge or obstacle you are facing toward the achievement of a particular goal...

➤ How can you frame this situation? What are your life principles, purpose, priorities and peculiarities that you want to take into account as you work to solve this?

➤ How can you focus on this issue? What do you need to do to concentrate and continually learn here?

➤ How can you be more flexible? Brainstorm several different possible ways to solve this.

Note: Try to be option-oriented, even allow for crazy ideas. Don't edit any until you review the list a second time. If solving this challenge involves responding to people differently, put down some alternative strategies for making mid-course corrections here as well.

Solution/Brainstorm

1.
2.
3.

People Strategies

1.
2.
3.

---

[i] Adapted from Rick Warren, "The Fax of Life," 29 September 1993.

Never Give Up, Never...Never Give Up!
Winston Churchill

10

Stay The Course

The Most Consistent
Leadership Principle in the World

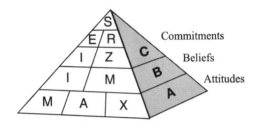

"When nothing seems to help, I go and look at a stonecutter, hammering away at his rock, perhaps a hundred times without as much as a crack showing in it. Yet at the hundred and first blow it will split in two, and I know it was not that blow that did it...but all that had gone before."

Jack Riis

One of the greatest tragedies of our day in materially wealthy countries is the insidious apathy and comfort that has settled in. Many of us have forgotten the reality of life.

Life is a challenge, a battle. It is not meant to be a playground where personal ease and satisfaction are the expected goals and results. Life is a precious resource to be invested for the good of self and others. It's not a sprint, but a marathon, requiring training, conditioning, courage, and a dogged commitment to *stay the course*. That requires that we fight the good fight, finish the course and focus on the future.

Fight the Good Fight

1. Practice Defensive Warfare

Begin your fight by identifying the forces that can throw you off course, make you second-guess your principles and keep you from fulfilling your mission.

➤ What cultural factors are attacking your "rightness living"? Remember, these are attitudes and thoughts that seep into your frame of reference. Do you really want them there? It's your choice. Do a reality check. Make a list.

➤ What about your own negative tendencies? Are you being held captive to your own passions? Articulate them and begin applying the principles in this book to take charge again.

➤ Where do you stand in the personal fight? Could other forces be moving you in the wrong direction? What are those forces, and how can you stand against them?

Inculcating the MAXIMIZERS will help protect you.

(1) The *Attitudes* principles protect your emotions

(2) The *Beliefs* principles protect your mind

(3) The *Commitments* principles protect your will.

Aggressively tending to the roots of your life helps guard against the inappropriate access of the world to your mind. And as you begin to reclaim the arena of your **attitudes, beliefs** and **commitments,** you will find renewed safety, energy, wisdom, and power to move into offensive warfare.

2. Practice Offensive Warfare

How will you know you have succeeded in the offensive warfare of life?

What will spell victory to you?

This is victory—to pick the fruit of maximum satisfaction and significance, knowing you're the best *you* can be. Daily, consistently and persistently build the MAXIMIZERS principles into your life. Your focus on the roots of "rightness living" will give you victory in the battle of life. Therefore, get active...get assertive...get energized...and get going! Deliberately get into the war!

Strategy. To win this offensive thrust, you need to develop a very specific strategy. It will not just happen. You must plan it. So, what is your strategy to take the offensive?

With what principles will you begin?

How will you schedule the application of these principles into your day-to-day activities? And how will you reinforce these principles in your life?

Begin with the *attitude* principles. Are you merely reacting to life or are you initiating according to the "Make Things Happen" principle? Are you "Achieving Personal Significance" by owning up to your soft spots and "X-ing Out the Negatives"?

Next, check your *belief* principles. Go back to your value system and articulate the nonnegotiable values in your life based on the chapter "Internalize Right Principles."

Then go to the "March to a Mission" chapter and develop your overall mission. This mission includes your purpose, vision, roles, and lifelong goals.

Finally, make appropriate *commitments*.

Maintain balance by "Integrating All of Your Life." Relate to the others around you by "Zeroing in on Caring for People" as your modus operandi.

Constantly "Energize Internally" as you build a character base and cultivate your spirit. Keep making mid-course corrections as you "Realign Rigorously."

Lastly, build the life craftsmanship skills of "Staying the Course" and not quitting.

Resources. Once you have determined your strategy, you must identify your resources. And since the battle is for your *mind*, your resources must be of a kind that will help you build the MAXIMIZERS principles into your mental framework.

What classic thinkers will you turn to for perspective and motivation? What current experts will you read?

What great speakers will you listen to during your commute?

Develop an Action Plan for success around which you organize these resources. This organization process will allow you to filter out irrelevant data, motivate you to look for specific, useful information, and help you build a life message that will give you the capability to help others based on your own life changes and growth.

Put together a resource organizer with tabs for each principle. Each tab should have space for articles, insights, quotations, exercises, and any other craftsmanship tools that will help you hone your understanding and application of these principles.

Make the search for wisdom and resources part and parcel of your daily life. Take the ten MAXIMIZERS principles and develop a code system to help you do this. I have done this and it helps me a great deal.

Principle one (Make Things Happen), for example, is coded as "M-1." Principle two (Achieve Personal Significance) is coded as "M-2," and so on. Whenever I read a book or article or have an insight, I mark it "M-1" or "M-2," and so on through "M-10."

Begin to apply this organizing approach to the majority of your conversations, reading time, and moments of reflection. Stop daily for some reflective time and write down your insights in your manual. And watch the internal power and fulfillment explode as you activate this process.

Keep growing. Read books, look for articles, study people, search for insights, reflect, pray, listen to tapes, watch videos, attend seminars, and find a mentor in authentic-life success.

(Over time I have collected and organized the best resources for each of these principles and have formed a curriculum that my associates and I communicate via workshops, conferences, audio/video tapes, and printed materials. If you would like information on these, refer to the end pages of this book.)

Team Unity. One final principle of offensive warfare is to cooperate as a unit. You must work together not only to cover each other's backs, but also to cohesively pursue and defeat the opposing forces in your lives. Whoever is part of your unit—whether family, friends, or business associates—it is critical that you work together with them. Whatever your battle, you can't do it alone. You are too vulnerable.

Applying these principles to your life will change the way you live. Your regular days will turn into extraordinary days. Your difficult days will become milestones of achievement and your normal life will turn into a life of success and rewards, beyond what you can imagine.

Finish the Course

How many projects have you started, but not finished? How often have you wanted to grow a garden, clean out the garage, exercise regularly or read more books only to become distracted by the everyday challenges of life or discouraged by a lack of results? Let's face it…you and I are busy with a million activities!

Finding the energy to try something new or get your creative juices flowing may sound more like work than fun, but you've already started to set some goals for your life. You've begun to discover your mission, your purpose, and to catch glimpses of exciting visions for your future. You don't want to let that go, do you? The principle skill to develop here is simply perseverance.

Here is a simple test for evaluating the degree of your perseverance developed by my friend, Bev Sallee, who asks these questions of herself and others.

> ➢ First, select a particular day; let's take yesterday.

> ➢ Second, read the statements below and disregard any that do not apply.

> ➢ Third, answer the remaining items *yes* or *no*, and count the number of *yes* answers.

1) First project for the day (in the office, at home, in school) earned my steady attention until it was completed.

2) My family knows that determination and perseverance are qualities that have characterized my life this day.

3) Aches and pains failed to deter me in my specific duties for the day.

4) While sentiment might have led me to relax discipline in my own life as well as toward my loved ones, I persevered in what seemed right to me.

5) Although at times I was disillusioned by others, and tempted to withdraw from such wholesome activities as church boards, and PTA, I continued to participate.

6) Encouragement in my chosen line of endeavor was clearly lacking today, but I persisted in doing that which I felt to be right.

7) Nothing deterred me from pursuing all of the details relative to my rightful duties for this day.

8) Despite a lack of genuine desire to continue my personal reading and reflection, I stuck with it in the certain knowledge that it was the right thing to do.

9) Today, I have kept in mind those deep healthy desires that I know to be the ones that cultivate the principle roots in my life.

Regardless of the circumstances never, ever give up!!!

Focus on the Future

Your future isn't as far away as you think. It begins right now. The question is how will others remember you in the future? Will they recognize your success? Will they only see the fruits of your labor or will they see the roots from which it all came?

When you begin to apply the principles in this book to your life on a daily basis you will change your future forever. The misdirected, unguided life that you could have led will be left behind in exchange for a life of purpose, vision, mission and accomplishment. You will touch others, some of whom you'll never meet. You'll be a better husband or wife, a better father or mother, a better friend and a better overall person. Your contribution to the world around you will be priceless and you'll create a legacy that can be passed on to future generations.

The choice is easy. We all want to make a difference and leave a lasting mark on the world. These simple principles will help you do just that. All it takes is consistency on your part and a willingness to change. The key is to *stay the course*. Through hard work and a shift in attitude you will see opportunities unfold. There is no reason for you not to have the life you truly desire.

As you focus on your future you will find strength and perseverance you didn't know you had. Your desire to be the best and achieve authentic success will drive you to fight against anything that will keep you from living out these principles. You will go from struggling to live each principle to struggling against anything that might move you off course. *You must keep moving forward.* Even when there are setbacks, you still have to carry on. Doing so will ensure your success and lead you toward the life about which you dream.

Everyone lives by a set of principles. They may be shaky, underhanded or well meaning yet misguided. The best principles are based on courage, honor, trust and generosity. The most successful people in the world have learned to live their lives based on principles that are right and true. You are invited to become one of these people. You have the ability, you have the drive, you have the knowledge and now you have the tools.

The principles set forth in this book will help you to live your *best* life. They will assist you in times of hardship and buoy you through rough waters. You have what it takes to live an authentic life. Now go out and achieve the success about which you've always dreamed. There is no reason for you to wait another moment. Start moving forward today and don't look back!

Never Give Up, Never...Never Give Up!
Winston Churchill

Action Steps

➤ Put to memory the MAXIMIZERS Acrostic and repeat it 4 times a day for the next 30 days.

➤ Identify which one of the four major areas of staying the course you struggle with the most. Identify one specific step to put feet to this area this week.

Make Things Happen

Achieve Personal Significance

X Out the Negatives

Internalize Right Principles

March to a Mission

Integrate All of Life

Zero In on Caring for People

Energize Internally

Realign Rigorously

S tay the Course

Impacting And Changing Cultures...
One Life At A Time!

Dr. Jenson's closing comments...

If you haven't developed your own philosophy of life (that is, organizing and guiding principles) I suggest you begin with the ten principles in this book, the MAXIMIZERS principles. In any given situation, you can use these as a grid.

Simply ask in your situation how the principle of "Make Things Happen" applies. Perhaps you'll conclude that you need to take the initiative to resolve the problem. After all, you are responsible; so be proactive! Then look at the principle of "Achieving Personal Significance." Perhaps you're holding back from making a certain decision because you lack confidence in yourself. This principle will help you adjust appropriately. You can follow the same process with all ten of the MAXIMIZERS principles.

If you will commit to *learning* and applying these principles in your own life you will realize tremendous results over the days, weeks, months and years ahead. Your greatest reward will be when you see how these principles have so impacted and changed your life that you then become motivated to *teach* each principle to those you influence.

The following chart provides a summary overview for each principle. Our organizations, our communities, our families, our children and the culture at large, need these principles *now* in order to have productive and successful lives of contribution that will set the stage for future generations!

MAXIMIZERS Principles

Make Things Happen
Teaches pro-active habit development and personal discipline.

This principle deals with eliminating a victim mentality and taking responsibility for developing the kind of discipline and new habits that lead to healthy thinking and job performance. This principle gives a person an understanding that they are in control of their own attitudes and actions.

Achieve Personal Significance

Teaches how to build a strong self-image.

This principle deals with the development of a healthy self-concept. The process of seeing your innate value and significance is balanced with the development of humility and the proper handling of criticism. Many personal conflicts and stress come from the improper view of oneself, which leads to an individual not maximizing his or her personal potential.

X Out the Negatives

Teaches how to deal with fears, problems and other difficulties.

This principle addresses what a positive attitude is and how to cultivate it in multiple areas of life. Negative situations can cause stress that can demoralize an individual's performance. Stress and negative situations managed properly can be turned into positive experiences as long as one can identify the weakness exposed and then strive to overcome them.

Internalize Right Principles

Teaches how to live a value driven lifestyle that reflects in work and at home.

Learning to build a value system around universal principles is crucial. Without such alignment the constant cognitive dissonance of wanting to do right but not doing it becomes stressful mentally, emotionally and physically.

March to a Mission   *Teaches how to build a sense of personal vision, mission and purpose for life.*

This principle addresses how to achieve the goals and vision that reflect in a person's ultimate desire. A clear sense of mission has been documented by research over the years as vital for personal wellness and preventing mental and physical illness. People lose hope when they don't have a sense of vision for their lives.

Integrate all of Life   *Teaches how to develop personal balance in attitudes, priorities and goals.*

When individuals get out of control and lose balance they become highly susceptible to distress, anger fear, depression and even burnout. There is a deep need to rebuild personal balance for individuals to maximize their productivity, overall job performance and personal contribution to the team.

Zero in on Caring for People   *Teaches how to listen, confront, empathize and coach.*

Research studies are quite clear…poor relationships (relational conflict) are highly stressful and lead ultimately to mental, emotional and physical illness. Clearly, the development of relational skills such as listening, empathizing, resolving conflict, anger management and encouraging others is essential to total health and productivity.

Energize Internally   *Teaches how to live a character-based lifestyle.*

People need to get back to this taproot principle of cultivating their spiritual moorings. As this inner life is cultivated and true character is developed an individual becomes "in sync." Our outward behavior begins to flow from our inward life. That is true health and is the ultimate power base for real wellness.

Realign Rigorously   *Teaches how to make the necessary mid-course corrections and to deal with constant change.*

Most people are constantly trying to prove the illusion that "life is supposed to be easy." This principle teaches people how to face the difficulties of life and how to make appropriate mid-course corrections. This learning process minimizes the distress of constant emotional and mental turmoil from worrying about problems.

Stay the Course   *Teaches the importance of staying focused and not quitting on the important issues.*

The American Management Association has indicated that the most universal principle of successful leaders is that they just don't quit. Those who succeed at healthy, dynamic whole lives fail often; but they fail forward. They learn how to stick with it and persist, focusing on the roots of building right principles into their lives.

FUTURE ACHIEVEMENT INTERNATIONAL®

Personal Leadership Solutions™...

Company Overview

Future Achievement International is a professional services company specializing in principle-centered Personal Leadership Solutions™ for organizations and individuals. Future Achievement's *Personal Leadership Solutions* consist of:

- Personal Leadership Assessment™
- Personal Leadership Coaching System™
- Personal Leadership Recruitment Profile™
- Personal Leadership Performance Management™

Most individuals and companies buying leadership products have engaged in short-term training and motivational events. Rarely is the impact of this effort measured or sustained. Future Achievement delivers leadership coaching solutions by helping the client define its leadership goals and systematically move individuals and organizations toward those goals.

Future Achievement's leadership programs, products and coaching services are currently distributed in over 40 countries. Please visit our website to learn more about how you can live a life of balance, productivity, impact and significance.

Please Visit Our Web Site
www.futureachievement.com